Richard Harries is the author of 30 books, mostly on the interface between Christian faith and wider culture, most recently *Haunted by Christ: Modern writers and the struggle for faith* (SPCK, 2018). One of his books was chosen by Anthony Burgess in *The Observer* as his book of the year, and another was shortlisted for the Michael Ramsay Prize. He is a Fellow of the Royal Society of Literature and an Honorary Fellow of the Academy of Medical Sciences. On his retirement as Bishop of Oxford (1987–2006), he was made a life peer (Lord Harries of Pentregarth) and he remains active in the House of Lords on human rights issues. His voice is well known to many as a result of his regular contributions to 'Thought for the Day' on the *Today* programme.

SEEING GOD IN ART

THE CHRISTIAN FAITH IN 30 IMAGES

RICHARD HARRIES

First published in Great Britain in 2020

Society for Promoting Christian Knowledge
36 Causton Street
London SW1P 4ST
www.spck.org.uk

British Library Cataloguing-in-Publication Data
A catalogue record for this book is available from the British Library

ISBN 978–0–281–08382–4
eBook ISBN 978–0–281–08383–1

1 3 5 7 9 10 8 6 4 2

Typeset by Fakenham Prepress Solutions, Fakenham, Norfolk NR21 8NL
First printed in Turkey by Mega Print
Subsequently digitally reprinted in Great Britain

eBook by Fakenham Prepress Solutions, Fakenham, Norfolk NR21 8NL

Produced on paper from sustainable forests

For Luke, Toby, Ben and Sophie

Contents

Contents

Part 3
IN CHRIST

Introduction

Sometimes when looking at a favourite painting I have thought to myself, 'If I could choose only a limited number of images to convey the essence of Christian faith, that is one I would include.' So I am grateful to Philip Law of SPCK, who suggested I select 30 such images for a book on that very theme. Of course, it would be wonderful to be able to choose one hundred works of art, but I have appreciated the discipline of being able to only include a smaller number for this book. Some of the works I have selected are well-known masterpieces. Others will be less familiar. All are images that, for me, mean a great deal.

The word 'image' is a very rich one in Christian thought. First, because we human beings are made in the divine image. In Greek the word is *eikon*. However, because the divine image has been defaced by our egoism, God came among us not only to reveal his heart of love but also to show us what it is to be a true human being. So it is Christ himself who is the real image of God, the prototype that we are called to reflect. Through this true image our own defaced image is to be restored.

At a third remove from Christ as the true image, and our vocation to be conformed to this image, Christian images, whether in mosaic, paint or any other medium, exist to help bring about our transformation into a true likeness. Such images, from the second and third centuries, very simple at that stage, exist in the Catacombs of Rome and elsewhere. At least since the time of Pope Gregory I (540–604), however, a difference of emphasis has arisen between Eastern and Western churches. In the West, the stress was on images as an educative tool in a largely illiterate population. In the East, Christians went beyond this and understood images in a more contemplative fashion. Among some people, this led to a fear of idolatry, and for more than two centuries the Church was racked by the iconoclastic controversy in which most Christian art of the time was destroyed. In 787, however, at the Seventh Ecumenical Council, the Church finally decided in favour of the legitimacy of Christian art. Indeed, the arguments used suggest that such art is not just an optional extra but essential to Christian understanding. Of course, they said, we cannot depict God, who is beyond any representation, but God has made himself visible in human form, the Word has become flesh. This we can and must convey. Furthermore, material things have been created good, so wood and paint can be used to witness to God's incarnation in Christ. So icons are not just there to look at and admire, they take us into the reality they seek to represent. As Rowan Williams has put it, 'The ikon, from very early on, is conceived as one of the means of grace, one of the means of spiritual transformation, *representing what it is meant to effect*.'[1] Although that has not been the familiar understanding of Western Christianity, this book has been designed to allow Western images, ancient and modern, and not just icons, not only to arrest the eyes and stimulate thought but also to lead the heart. So each reflection ends with a very short prayer.

In the 900 words or so of reflection I have written in response to each image, I have tried to explicate what it means for me in terms of Christian truth. I have also tried to face, head-on, the questions that inevitably arise in our sceptical age.

I have chosen images from both East and West, and from almost all periods of Christian history. A self-imposed limitation has been to choose only one image from each artist. The work of some artists, such as Giotto or Rembrandt, feature so many paintings on the Christian faith that they could warrant a large volume on their own. My other limitation is that, with one exception, the works chosen are from Europe, so there could be other volumes reflecting the Christian art of Africa, China, the United States and other countries.

The images are arranged in three broad areas: in time, in history and in Christ. The first section, in time, deals with the unimaginable, incomprehensible creation of the universe, with its teeming life culminating in us human beings – matters that can only be expressed in simple visual images. These are not, of course, depictions of historical incidents, but symbols of fundamental spiritual realities. The second section, in history, concerns the special vocation of the Jewish people as it comes to be focused on Jesus. The third section, in Christ, explores the experience of Christians being incorporated into the divine life. This includes prayer, 'Christian mindfulness', and the Eucharist.

The Christian story gives us the most sublimely beautiful account it is possible to imagine of what it is to be a human being, of why we are here and what God has in mind for us. For two thousand years it has captured the imagination of whole cultures, and of some people in almost every culture, giving meaning and purpose even through great suffering. When Rowan Williams became Archbishop of Canterbury, he said his hope was that the Christian faith would once again capture the imagination of our culture. I share that hope, so even if people are not able, at the moment, to share the faith, they will at least feel the force of its attraction and understand why it has inspired so many lives.

Part 1
IN TIME

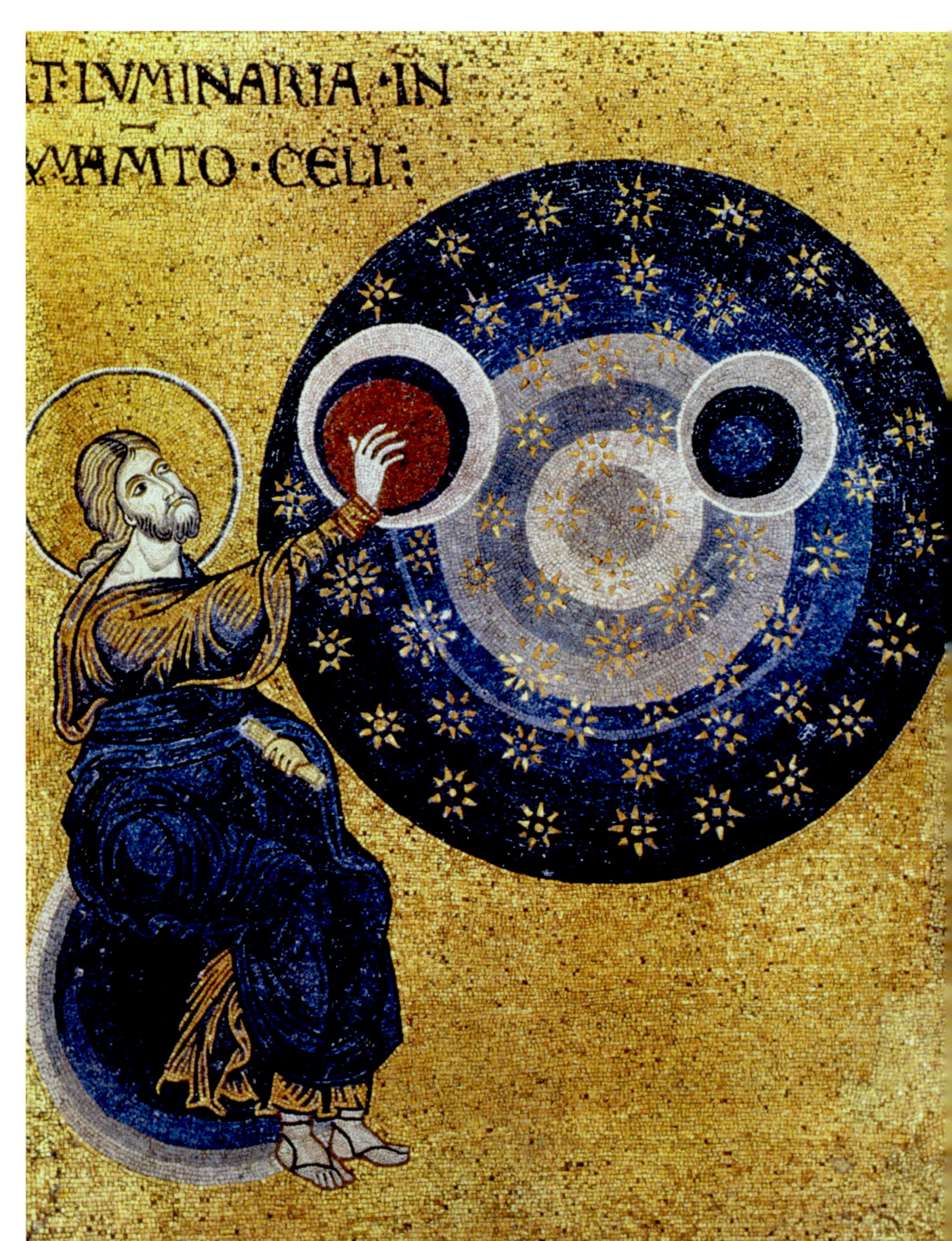
T·LVMINARIA·IN
FIRMAMTO·CELI:

1

'Let there be . . .'

The creation of the sun, moon and stars, twelfth-century mosaic

This is one of the many superb mosaics in Monreale Cathedral, in Palermo, Sicily,[2] that tell the Christian story from creation onwards. It depicts the creation of the stars, the sun and moon, and the planets (Genesis 1.1–5, 14–19). In God's left hand is a scroll that symbolizes the ruling principles on which the universe operates or, as we would say, the fundamental laws of nature. A similar scheme of mosaics can be found in the nearby Palatine chapel in the royal palace.

As mentioned in the Introduction, there was a difference between East and West in their understanding of Christian art. In these Monreale mosaics, the two approaches come together. The Christian story is told from creation onwards, but each scene has an iconic quality that draws us to reflect and pray.

The creation of the universe is of course beyond anything our tiny human minds can picture, but the artist here has made a bold attempt to put it in symbolic form. All stems from God's great 'Let there be . . .', indicated by his outstretched arm. This 'Let there be . . .' runs throughout the first chapter of the Bible. God's hand not only brings things into being, it is a hand that blesses. It reminds us of other words from Genesis: 'All that he made was very good'.

We might think it childlike to picture God in these terms, but however sophisticated our attempt to visualize the moment when matter appeared *ex nihilo,* out of nothing, it will still only be a human picture of what is beyond our comprehension. In a way, the more childlike the better, for it then brings home to us the fact that we are using human images to depict what cannot be imagined.

One of the great scientific achievements of recent decades is that the created side of this unimaginable moment of creation can be mapped out in mathematical terms. Advanced instruments for measurement, together with very high-level maths, can take astronomers and mathematical physicists back to the first few seconds of the explosion of energy we call the 'big bang': the point from which the universe has since expanded ever outwards at the speed of light. It was the Catholic priest and astronomer Georges Lemaître who first noted in 1927 that an expanding universe could be traced back in time to an originating single point; since then, scientists have built on his idea of cosmic expansion.

We now know that the universe is 13.8 billion years old. It contains 10 billion galaxies, and each galaxy contains about 100 billion stars. This means that there are something like one billion trillion stars in the observable universe. Earth is of course a planet of one star, the Sun, which is part of one galaxy, the Milky Way. Time and space, as we know them, begin at this point. No wonder the psalmist cries out, 'The heavens declare the glory of God: and the firmament sheweth his handywork' (Psalm 19.1, KJV). No wonder poets in every age, like Gerard Manley Hopkins, have written words such as 'The world is charged with the grandeur of God. / It will flame out, like shining from shook foil.' We do not know God in himself. We only know him in and through the secondary causes of which he is the first cause. We know him in the wonder we feel when we look up at the night sky.

What is fascinating about the brilliant scientific work done on the origin of the universe in recent decades is the way its truth has been yielded up through mathematical equations of great beauty. Mathematicians sometimes marvel at the way amazing complexity can be brought together in equations of such simplicity and elegance. Not unrelated to this phenomenon is the equally amazing capacity of the human mind to explore and map out the universe in this way. All this bears out what the Church has long taught, both about the fundamental beauty of the universe and the natural laws on which it is based, and our God-given reason, which is able to recognize and understand these laws.

No scientific exploration can locate God in this process, for God is not a thing in the world of things. He is the uncreated source of all things. There is only one place where we can discover God, and that is in ourselves. We discover him as the root of our own existence, the source from whom our being flows. But because the fundamental energy that keeps us in being is one with the fundamental energy that brought the universe into being in the first place, God is the root of the universe as well. Moment by moment I am held in being – and if I am, so is the universe as a whole.

That is what is really meant when we say that God is creator, and that is why it would not affect this belief if some scientific reality could be found to exist before the 'big bang'. That too would exist only because of the uncreated source of all energy. Nor would it affect the issue if it were discovered that there is a multiverse. Before the theory of the 'big bang' was shown to be true, a widely held view was that the universe was being continuously created. Even now it could be that the 'big bang' was just one in a series of explosions and contractions. If this were shown to be so, again it would not affect the fundamental Christian belief, shared by Jews and Muslims, that whatever the process whereby we come into being, it depends on an uncreated source of all processes. The basis of this belief is the lived faith of believers, that they are dependent on God as they are on the air they breathe and the ground they walk on.

Unimaginable God, you have set us in this universe of awesome grandeur. Moment by moment you hold it in existence. You are the fount from whom my being flows. On you I depend, in you I trust.

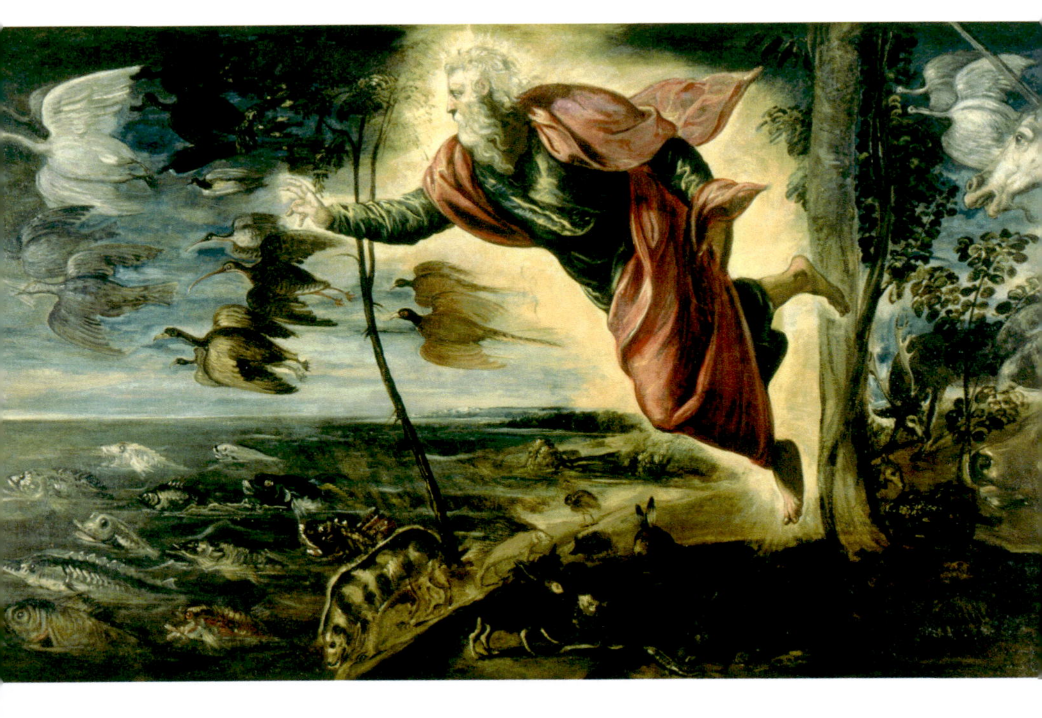

2

Animals come into being

Jacopo Tintoretto, *Creation of the Animals, 1551–52*

This painting of God creating the animals, based on Genesis 1.20–25, exudes energy and vitality. All is on the move, a movement set in motion by the right hand of God who is himself moving, almost chasing the birds into existence.

We now know that animals were not created all at once but came into existence over a long period of evolution. The earth was formed about 5.54 billion years ago, and there is undisputed evidence that life was present on earth from about 3.5 billion years ago. Life has evolved very, very gradually over that period. Against that background, the age of the dinosaurs, which ended 66 million years ago, is relatively recent. When the theory of evolution was first put forward, thoughtful Christians found no contradiction between this and the biblical account in Genesis 1.20–25. They argued that God works through secondary causes over a long period of time. He does not just make the world. He does something even more wonderful; he makes the world make itself.

God is, by definition, the underlying, fathomless first cause of all secondary causes. He is not another thing in the world of things. He does not take up or threaten our space in any way. He works in and through all secondary causes in accord with the fundamental rules of nature. The twin secondary causes through which evolution takes place are genetic mutation and natural selection. All living organisms give rise from time to time to random genetic mutations. Those which adapt to their environment survive and those that don't perish. Those which survive produce genes that will also survive in the particular environment. These random mutations allow new forms of existence to emerge, and the stability provided by the need to adapt to the environment means that new forms will be preserved. It is this combination of freedom and stability which is creative. The phrase 'survival of the fittest' sometimes makes us think of a phrase commonly ascribed to Tennyson that nature is 'red in tooth and claw'. Survival of the fittest, however, simply means survival of those forms of life that are best adapted to their environment, whether air or earth or water, hot or cold, light or dark. When watching wildlife programmes on television, for example, it can be distressing to see one beautiful animal tear another apart. We wonder whose side God is on, the desperately hungry tiger or the fearful antelope. There is a mystery here that we cannot fathom, but we should avoid projecting human emotions on to animals. Each follows the law of its own nature, and in being itself reflects the divine glory.

In Coleridge's poem about the Ancient Mariner, the Mariner is in despair. Then he looks over the side of the ship and sees some water snakes swimming around. These shiny, slimy creatures would normally make most of us shudder, but the Mariner cries out:

> O happy living things! no tongue
> Their beauty might declare:
> A spring of love gushed from my heart,
> And I blessed them unaware:
> Sure my kind saint took pity on me,
> And I blessed them unaware.

> The self-same moment I could pray . . .

It was the wonder and beauty of creation, even if what he saw was not conventionally attractive, that released the Mariner from his sense of guilt and self-absorbed depression.

We human beings have only been around for a fraction of a second compared with the long stretch of time in which other forms of animal life dominated the earth. So nature is not just a backdrop to human life, as our forebears thought, but significant in itself, for itself. Here is the creative exuberance of the divine in full play. Here is the glory of God revealed in countless forms. Our forebears thought that human beings, in dominating the earth, could do what they liked with it. We now rightly reject this and understand our role to be that of stewards, taking care of our environment.

When we look at this painting by Tintoretto (1518–94), we see the sea teeming with fish and the air full of birds. We now know that stocks of many kinds of fish are drastically depleted and numerous species of birds and animals are in grave danger of extinction. Saving the richness and variety of creation for future generations has rightly become a major priority. What is interesting about this huge shift in our attitude is what it brings home to us about the intrinsic value of the natural world. Although there are important scientific arguments in favour of preserving our natural habitat because our future depends on the existence of a great variety of plants and species, there is also a sound instinct at work that recognizes this diverse richness as valuable in itself, for itself. As noted earlier, Genesis 1.31 affirms creation in the most wonderful words: 'And God saw all that he had made, and, behold, it was very good.'

We bless you O God for creation, at once fearful and beautiful, so richly varied and so intricate in detail.

Give us the will to preserve its richness and variety for those who come after us.

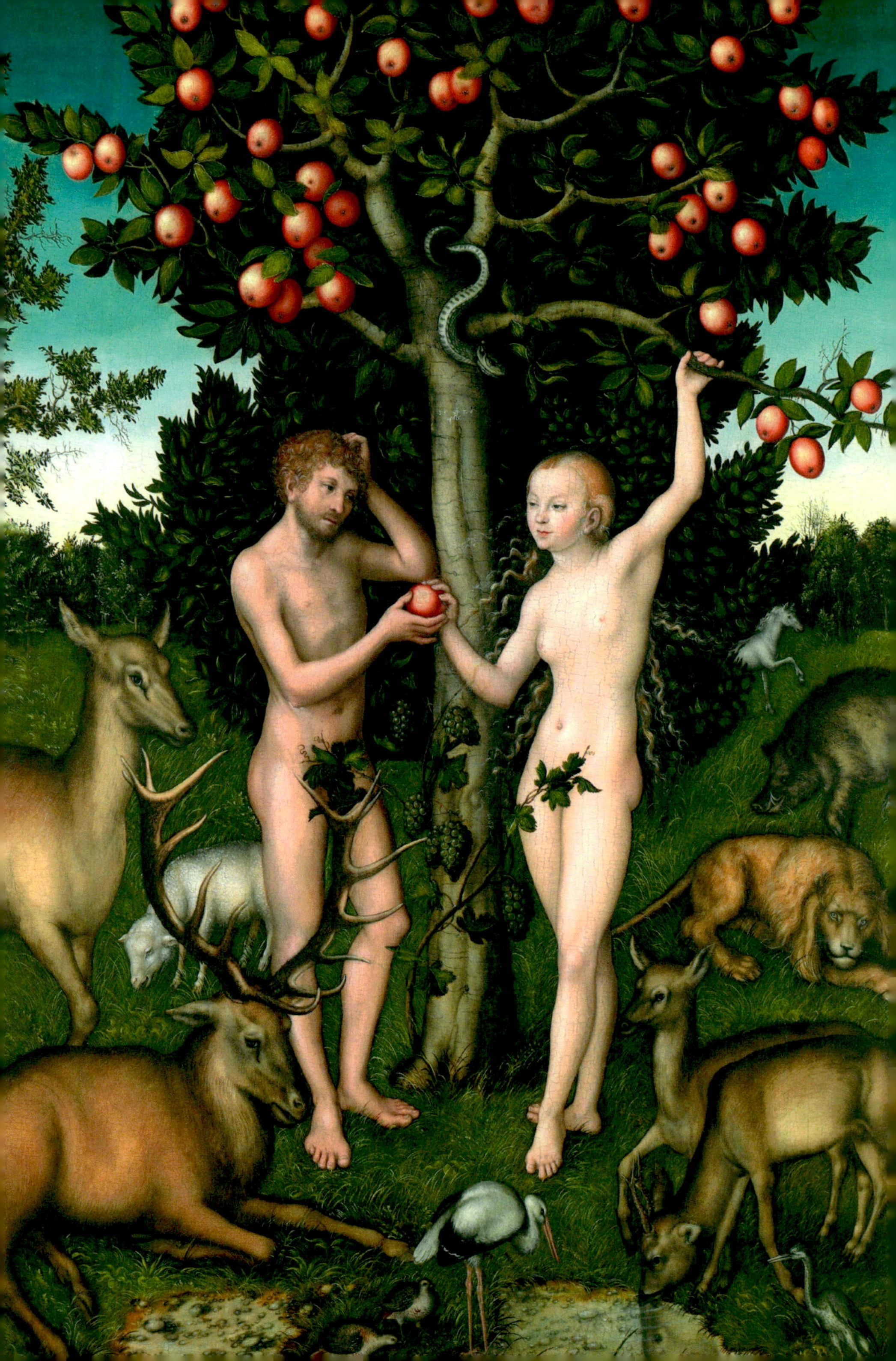

3
The image of God
Lucas Cranach the Elder, *Adam and Eve*, 1526

Genesis 1.27 says, 'God created human beings in his own image. In his own image he created them. Male and female he created them.' In other words, we are made in the image of God not as solitary individuals, but with others, in particular as male and female. In this painting, Adam and Eve, dwelling in the innocent paradise of Eden, are confronted by a choice: whether or not to eat the apple. The evolutionary process discussed in the previous two reflections comes to a climax in human beings, who are able to make conscious choices that shape their future.

The bodies of Adam and Eve are wondrous and beautiful. Wondrous because the complex workings of the body are so miraculous. The body contains 37.2 trillion cells and each cell contains 10^{14} atoms – that is 100 trillion. This is not to speak of the 39 trillion bacteria that are now regarded as essential to our health. Each element, atom, cell and organism goes on being itself while combining in complex ways to produce ever more complex combinations, until you and I emerge and reflect on what it is all about. No surprise, then, that the psalmist exclaimed, 'I will give thanks unto thee, for I am fearfully and wonderfully made' (Psalm 139.13). In the painting, Adam and Eve are beautiful because, when we love someone, we see them as beautiful however they are shaped physically, and that is how we should see others, because that is how God sees us all.

Adam and Eve are looking at an apple and deciding whether or not to eat it. Life is made up of choices, from the moment we get up and decide what to have for breakfast, to the moment we decide when to go to bed. Most decisions are small, but some are life-changing, such as the job we choose to do or the person we should marry. This capacity to reflect and make conscious choices is part of what we mean by being made in the image of God. Such choices have consequences both for ourselves and others, consequences for good and ill. In short, they are moral choices. They both shape us into being a particular kind of person, and affect the well-being of others.

We are made in the image of God – but more than this, the Christian faith teaches us that we are called to grow into his likeness. That is, we are called to grow in love for others and for God himself. This is a process that goes on all through our life. When we are born we have a strong instinct to survive. The baby reaches out for her mother's breast and later goes after what she wants without thought for others. This desire to look after oneself is an essential part of nature, otherwise no baby would survive. But as we grow up we become aware of others, and come to see that like us they have needs which must be taken into account. Our choices are often about how far we are prepared to take those needs into consideration, even sometimes at the expense of our own immediate desires. For very many mothers this self-forgetful love for their young baby comes naturally. But for most of us, for a great deal of the time, it is a struggle to take others fully into account. It is a huge advantage to this process of growing awareness of others if we have grown up in a warm and loving family, and a great disadvantage if we have grown up in a mean and selfish one.

At the same time as we grow into moral maturity, there are moments when we reflect on what life is all about. For some there are occasions when they think there might be a good creator, or even moments when they pray. These will not usually be like a great light in the eyes blinding us, but more like a candle glimmering in the darkness, enabling us to pick our way. As we allow ourselves to be guided by this light we grow in the likeness of God. Then it is not our choices alone that determine the future; those choices are now illuminated by the light of God. So the process of decentring the ego is twofold, and goes on in relation both to other people and God.

The biblical text quoted at the beginning of this reflection says that we are made in the image of God not as solitary individuals, but with others, in particular as male and female. It is in and through our relationships, especially with those closest to us, that we live out what it is to be made in the image of God and called to grow into his likeness.

Human beings are the crown and climax of creation. In us creation becomes articulate. In us the natural world, which praises God just by being itself, finds a voice. In this painting by Cranach (1472–1553) the natural world is there in all its wondrous beauty, but it is in Adam and Eve that the animal world finds its fulfilment. As Eucharist Prayer G in the Church of England's *Common Worship* reads:

> From the beginning you have created all things
> and all your works echo the silent music of your praise.
> In the fullness of time you made us in your image,
> the crown of all creation.
> You give us breath and speech, that with angels and
>   archangels
> and all the powers of heaven
> we may find a voice to sing your praise.

We could then pray:

> We bless you O God for our creation, preservation and all the blessings of this life.

> Guide me in the right way, that I may make right choices both for myself and the well-being of others.

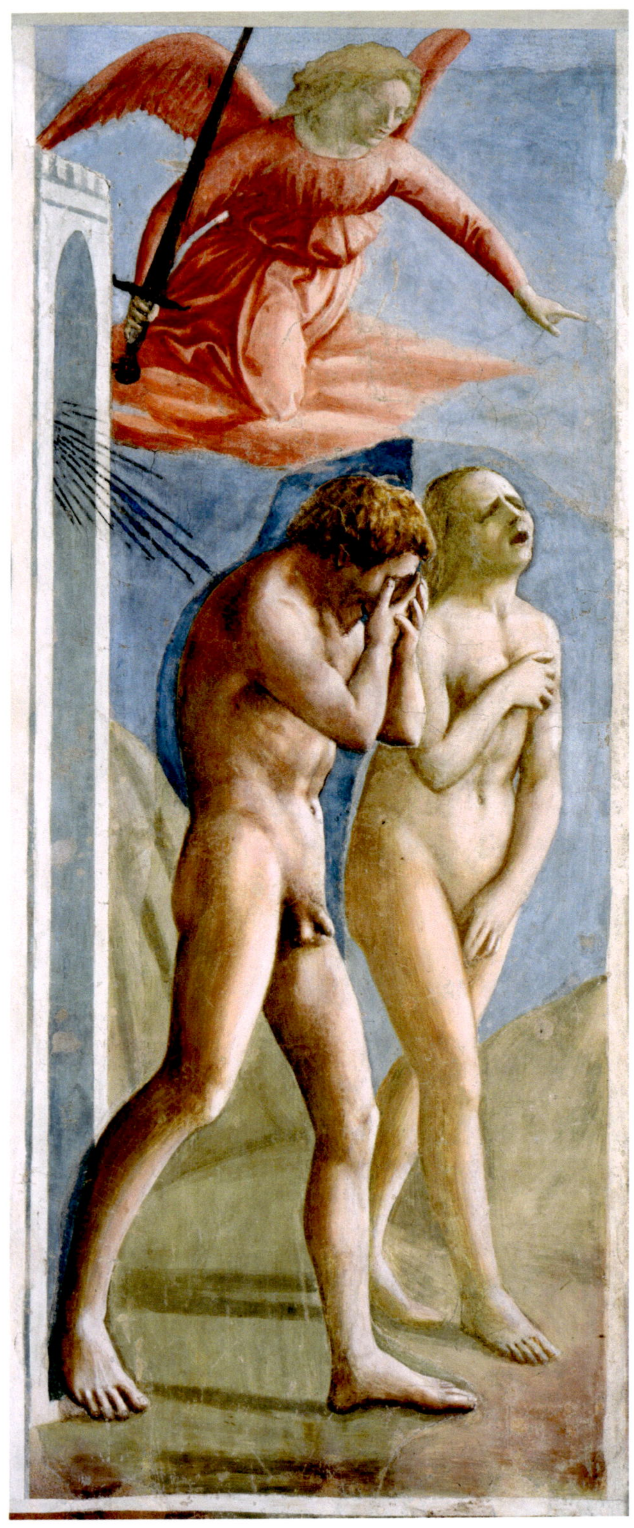

4

'Some natural tears they dropped'

Masaccio, *The Expulsion from Eden*, c. 1425

In this painting by Masaccio (1401–28/9), who transformed Florentine painting through his use of perspective, Adam and Eve are seen distraught as they leave the garden of Eden. Adam buries his head in his hands, Eve looks heavenwards. Both are naked and vulnerable. The angel driving them out makes it clear there is no way back.

The story of Adam and Eve, which appears in Genesis 3, is a myth told by our forebears to account for some of the distressing features of human life, such as the pain of childbirth and the hard manual labour necessary even to survive. One of these features is the fact that there is so much evil and suffering in the world. The world we know seems such a long way from the paradise we might dream of. In this painting it is the loss of the innocent goodness of Eden that is so painful to the couple.

The Christian faith teaches us that something has gone badly wrong in human development. To use the old terminology, we are all affected by 'original sin': we are born into and shaped by an environment that is out of kilter. Not original guilt, it should be noted. We are not to be blamed for this, but we have to be realistic and take it into account in all our doings, both personal and political, in ourselves and others. At a personal level it demands of us complete honesty in searching out our real feelings and motives, and being open about them before God. If we do this, we will probably find in ourselves the seeds of the faults for which we criticize others.

As a result there is no place for self-righteous moralizing. At a political level, it means that in any political arrangement we need to make sure that there are checks and balances in place to ensure that no one person or group can obtain power and suppress all opposition. We can dream of creating a perfect society on earth, but if we try to achieve this without taking into account our human tendency to pursue our own interests at the expense of others, sometimes ruthlessly, we will quickly slide into despotism or disintegrate into warring factions. Christian realism says that there will always be competing factions and we have to manage them in such a way that they do not destroy everything. At the same time we must not give up working for a better society, so far as it is possible under the conditions of sinful human existence.

The most moving comment on our loss of an earthly paradise comes right at the end of John Milton's *Paradise Lost*:

> Some natural tears they dropped, but wiped them soon;
> The world was all before them, where to choose
> their place of rest, and Providence their guide:
> They hand in hand with wand'ring steps and slow,
> through Eden took their solitary way.

There is real sadness in life, but still we have to get on with living. 'Some natural tears they dropped, but wiped them soon'. And although the loss of Eden is tragic, life still has much to offer. Life is before us and we have the task of choosing how we will live it. 'The world was all before them, where to choose / their place of rest'. This is a solitary way that involves loneliness, but we can take it alongside others. 'They hand in hand with wand'ring steps and slow / through Eden took their solitary way'. And we can do it as they did, 'with Providence their guide'.

In my reflection on the first painting in this book I said that, while we cannot see God directly in the 'big bang', we can know God to be the ground of our own being, at the centre of our personal life, and knowing him there we know he is the ground of all that exists, for we are all part of the same created energy and matter. In a similar way we cannot see God in the evolutionary process that was outlined in response to the second painting. What we see at work is a process of genetic mutation and natural selection leading to ever higher forms of life, culminating in the emergence of human beings. But if we can discern something of divine leading in our own life, then it is only logical to posit that same divine leading in the evolutionary process, for we are a result of that process. So it is that Adam and Eve, as they wipe away their tears and make their way through life, with all its struggle and suffering, do so 'with Providence their guide'. This providence does not overrule their natural processes of decision making but works through them. In the believer's experience, decisions made before God and in response to what are believed to be his purposes for us, will be wise and in the end turn out to be right.

Adam and Eve felt that life was hard, and in Masaccio's painting their faces are anguished. Some words written by John Henry Newman when he too was finding life difficult, and the future uncertain, seem very appropriate at such times:

Lead, kindly Light, amid the encircling gloom
Lead thou me on;
The night is dark, and I am far from home,
Lead thou me on.
Keep thou my feet; I do not ask to see
The distant scene; one step enough for me.

Part 2

IN HISTORY

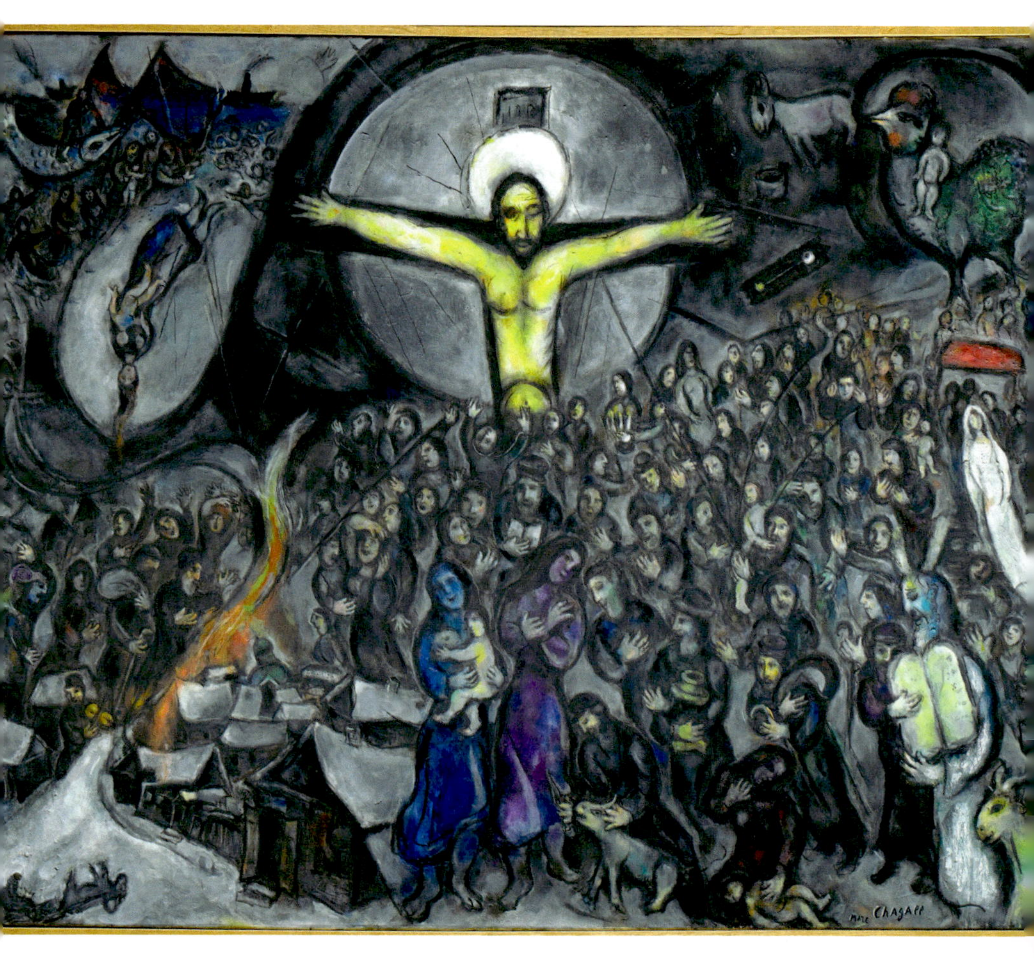

5

Liberated into freedom

Marc Chagall, *Exodus*, 1952

In this painting Marc Chagall (1887–1985) depicts God shepherding his people over the Red Sea as they escape from Egypt (see Exodus 14.10–31). What is startling is that God is pictured as the Christ of an Orthodox icon. Chagall's own faith was a mystical Judaism, but he was born and brought up in the small town of Vitebsk, now in Belarus but then under Russian and, later, Soviet control. The village had a number of impressive churches and Chagall was haunted by the figure of Christ depicted in Orthodox icons; it is this face that appears in a number of his own paintings.

The images and reflections in Part 1 concerned the whole universe at the start of time: stars, animals and every woman and man. In the next few paintings the focus narrows to a particular people and a specific history. It is natural for us to think that, if there is a wise and loving power behind the universe, all human beings will be loved equally and given an equal chance to know and be known. And that is the case. Something of God can be known by everyone through the things he has made, especially ourselves, and he has given us enough spiritual light within to discern this. We can all come to know ourselves as creatures set in an awesome world that we ourselves did not make, and with some capacity to discern right from wrong.

But this does not give us very clear knowledge. Besides, if something drastic has gone wrong in human development the effects will be present not only in our relationships with one another but in our whole understanding of God. Pursuing our own interests we will be likely to imagine the god we most want or the one we most fear; in other words we will make an idol created in our own likeness. The living God does not want to leave us with such vague and sometimes distorted notions. So he has chosen a particular people – the Jews – in order to reveal his purpose more clearly. If a house is on fire and people can only be rescued one at a time, a choice has to be made about who will be first. The Jewish people stressed that it was not because they were stronger, cleverer or better than other nations that they were chosen, nor was it because God preferred them to others. It was simply because this was what God in his inscrutable wisdom chose to do. Moreover, this election to be a special people carried with it frightening responsibilities.

The first story that shaped – and still shapes – the Jewish people is the deliverance from oppression in Egypt, and it is the culmination of that event that Chagall depicts in this painting. The Israelites had been forced into slavery and ever-increasing burdens inflicted on them, but God raised up a leader, Moses, to rescue them and bring them to where they could live in freedom. This event has been continually retold in Jewish life, especially at the annual Passover. In Chagall's painting can be seen various Jewish figures and symbols, especially the Torah (which is depicted in the bottom right-hand corner), while the Holy Scriptures are being carried, keeping alive the theme of God as our deliverer.

The idea of deliverance became central to Jewish thinking. Recalling the great rescue from Egypt, they later looked to God to deliver them from the oppressive nations around them, and especially from exile in Babylon in the sixth century before Christ. Later they looked to a time when God would deliver them from all forms of evil and suffering.

The Christian faith also looks back to the rescue of God's people from Egypt and thinks of God as the great deliverer. For Christians this is brought into even sharper focus in the life, death and resurrection of Jesus, who came to overcome even death itself on behalf of all humanity. Not surprisingly this belief has had great resonance for oppressed peoples down the ages, not least for the enslaved black population in the United States in whose music the theme is powerfully reflected. More recently it has had resonance in the liberation theology of Christians working alongside the poor in South America and elsewhere.

If deliverance is a defining image, this means that religion is not in the first place about believing certain things to be true or behaving in a particular way. It is about experiencing the beginning of a change in one's life. For some people this happens dramatically, when they find God's grace helping them to overcome an addiction to alcohol or drugs or promiscuity. Others find in it a release from crippling anxiety or guilt or a sense of worthlessness. Still others experience the operation of God's grace in more gradual ways, taking them away from self-preoccupation to a greater focus on others and their needs; and to God and what he might want of us.

This is not meant to be just an individual experience, but one involving the whole community. As the Jewish people know they are expected to live out God's good purpose in a life together marked by justice and mercy, so Christians look to the Christian community to manifest similar characteristics in congregations of mutual love and support.

There are many evils we would like the world to be delivered from: poverty, cruelty, war, oppression and injustice, for a start. Christians believe that this process must begin within each one of us, as we discover the deliverance, liberation and freedom that comes through Christ in the service of God. It begins within but does not stop there. It will be manifest in trying to do what we can to alleviate human suffering and promote the well-being of others.

St Augustine wrote a prayer that I have always found helpful:

O Thou, who art the light of the minds that know thee,
the life of the souls that love thee
and the strength of the wills that serve thee.
Help us so to know thee that we may truly love thee.
So to love thee that we may fully serve thee,
Whom to serve is perfect freedom.

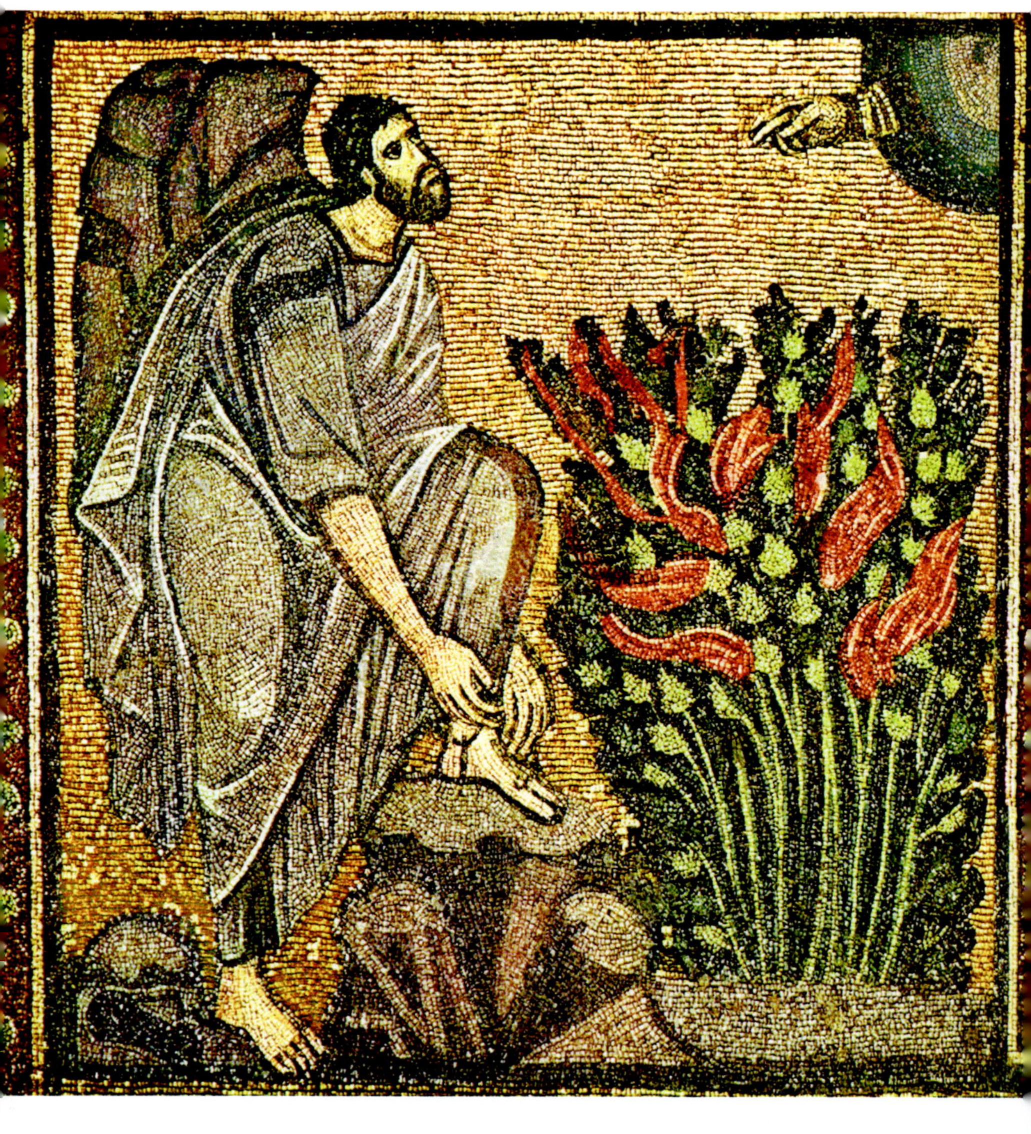

6

The way of life required of God's people

Moses before the burning bush, sixth-century mosaic

As mentioned in the previous reflection, the key figure in Israel's deliverance from Egypt was Moses. This sixth-century mosaic from St Catherine's Monastery in Sinai depicts a pivotal moment in Moses' life. It shows him taking his sandals off before a bush that was burning but not turning to ashes, while God spoke to him from the bush. Another mosaic in the same church shows him receiving the divine law from heaven.

A voice from the burning bush tells Moses that he is to lead his people out of Egypt. He asks what he should say when the people enquire who has sent him, and he is told: '"I am who I am", tell them I am has sent you to them' (Exodus 3.14). This indicates that for our limited human minds there is an ultimate unknownness about God, before whom there can only be reverent silence. Indeed the great eighth-century bishop John of Damascus wrote that 'What God is in himself is totally unknowable and incomprehensible.' The transliteration of the divine name is YHWH, and Jews came to regard this as too sacred to be uttered.

What God does reveal, however, is the way of life he wants his people to follow. The mosaic of Moses in St Catherine's shows a hand coming out of the dark cloud of God, what is sometimes referred to as the cloud of unknowing,[3] handing Moses the revealed way of life.

Moses is told that there is a solemn binding agreement (a covenant) between God and his people. On God's side it means total faithfulness, and in return he asks of them a particular way of life revealed in the Torah. At the heart of this are the Ten Commandments, the basic rules of civilized living that are essential for any society if it is to hold together (Deuteronomy 5.6–21).

At one time these would have been written out on boards and set beside the altar of many Anglican churches, and would have been well known to everyone. Now, in *Common Worship*, the Church of England's most popular prayer book, they are recited on Sundays in Advent and Lent. At other times Jesus' summary of the law is used:

'You shall love the Lord your God with all your heart and with all your soul and with all your mind.' This is the great and first commandment. And a second is like it: 'You shall love your neighbour as yourself.' On these two commandments depend all the Law and the Prophets.
(Matthew 22.37–40)

Christians believe that the solemn binding agreement with God's people in Judaism has been renewed and opened out to all people in Jesus Christ as the new covenant. At the heart of this new covenant is the belief that God is fully for us, is on our side through thick and thin, as revealed in the total self-giving presence of Christ. On our side we are called to respond in trust, and this trust is to find obedient expression in following Jesus and loving one another.

The attitude of Christians to Jews has for most of history been appalling and deeply shaming. The relationship has now been rethought, and this finds expression in the Church of England's prayer for Good Friday, in which what Christians ask for themselves, they ask for Jews as well:

Let us pray for God's ancient people, the Jews,
the first to hear his word:
    for greater understanding between Christian and Jew,
    for the removal of our blindness and bitterness of heart,
that God will grant us grace to be faithful to his covenant
and to grow in the love of his name.[4]

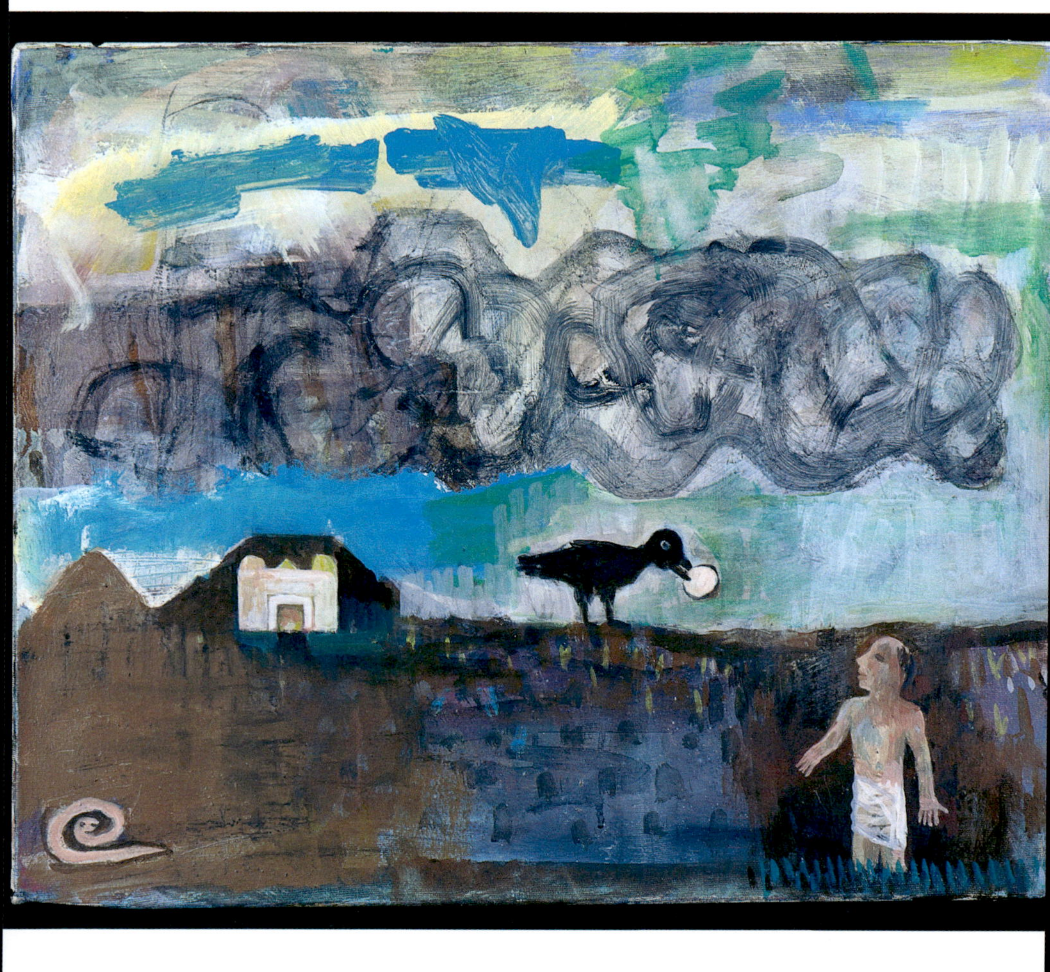

7

Prophetic critique

Albert Herbert, *Elijah Being Fed by a Raven*, 1992

In the Hebrew Bible, the first strand of divine disclosure is the law or way of life, which was to guide and shape God's people in their life together. The second strand is the prophetic critique of the people for their failure to live up to this law, which they had agreed to obey. The figure who, more than any other, stands as a symbol of this strand is the prophet Elijah, who lived in the ninth century before Christ in the northern kingdom of Israel. We think of prophets as being fierce, rugged figures, but in this painting by Albert Herbert (1925–2008) Elijah is shown as very vulnerable, a balding, middle-aged man. The scene shows him being fed by a raven in the desert (1 Kings 17.2–16).

In the eighth century there arose a number of prophets who were highly critical of the society around them. They slammed the greed of the rich at the expense of the poor, the emptiness of religion, and corrupt judges. All this, they said, was contrary to what God had asked of them, and without this fundamental social justice their religion was worthless. Isaiah, Amos, Hosea and Micah repeated the same message in different forms, a message well summed up in the following words:

He has told you, O mortal, what is good;
And what does the Lord require of you
But to do justice, and to love kindness
And to walk humbly with your God?
(Micah 6.8)

At the same time as criticizing their contemporaries, these prophets often held out a vision of a different future when God would bring about a new, better world. This is a marked feature of the book of Isaiah from chapter 40 onwards and is succinctly summarized by Jeremiah, who lived in the sixth century before Christ. He said that the days were coming when God would make a new covenant, or solemn binding agreement, with his people. At that time, God promised,

> I will put my law within them, and I will write it on their hearts, and I will be their God, and they shall be my people. No longer shall they teach one another, or say to each other, 'Know the LORD', for they shall all know me, from the least of them to the greatest, says the LORD.
> (Jeremiah 31.33–34, NRSV)

To stand up for justice in our skewed world requires courage. In so many countries, to work for basic human rights such as freedom of religion or speech or the press puts a person's life at risk. It is a frightening thing to do. That is why I like the way Albert Herbert has depicted the prophet as utterly vulnerable. The picture also shows his total dependence on God's grace to help him go through with what he has set out to do. In the story Elijah has nothing to eat, but God supports him by getting the ravens to feed him. A Christian looking at this painting will notice that the bread with which Elijah is being fed is the round, sacramental bread of the Eucharist, the very life of Christ that sustains and nurtures our Christian life.

During the 1960s Albert Herbert was teaching at St Martin's School of Art, at the height of American Abstractionism. Although he could produce effective works in this style, he became dissatisfied with it and used to go down into the basement to teach himself to draw like a child again. This child's view of the world produced some remarkable paintings on religious themes, of which this is just one.

We are reminded of Christ's words that to enter the kingdom of God we have to receive it like a child.

A child quickly notices when something is unfair. That child's eye is needed all through life to keep us aware of how we have turned God's good world into a place of such massive unfairness. We may not be able to do a great deal, but rather than simply resigning ourselves to it, we can try to do something, however small. That can sometimes be scary, and we may feel as vulnerable as Elijah in this painting. We need help. The painting says that God's grace is available and can come to us in unexpected ways. The scene is overshadowed by a large black cloud, which all of us will be conscious of in some periods of our life, when we feel in a bad way or the world seems in a terrible state. In the painting a mysterious religious-looking building can also be seen. Perhaps this is a secret place in our heart we have to enter, for behind the hill in which the building is set the sky looks brighter.

> Grant us, O God, honesty to see the world as it is,
> courage to protest against its wrongs,
> strength to put right what we can
> and your grace in all things.

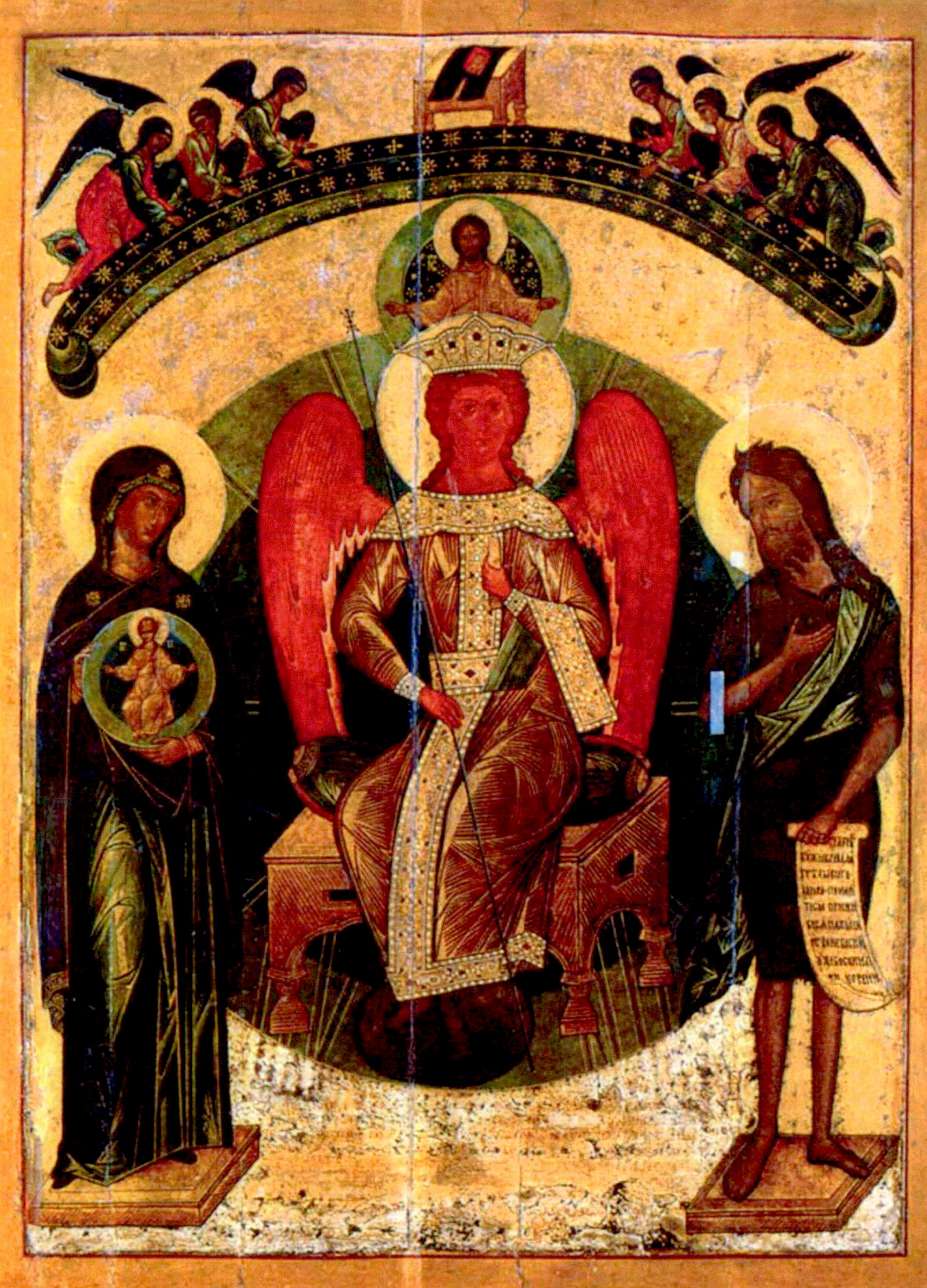

8

Divine wisdom

Holy Wisdom, sixteenth-century icon

In this icon in the cathedral in Novgorod (one of the main centres of icon painting in Russia during the sixteenth century), John the Baptist, the forerunner who prepares the way for Christ, stands on one side. On the other is Mary, holding the Christ child within a circle. The main focus however, below a small figure of Christ in his traditional depiction, is on the large figure of Christ as divine wisdom.

The disclosure of God's good purpose for humanity to and through the Jewish people has three strands to it. First is the divine law given to Moses, laying out the basic moral principles by which the community is to be guided. Second is the prophetic critique of the people for their failure to live by these rules, even though they had promised to obey them. Third is the divine wisdom – the wisdom, both rational and practical, that is reflected in the ordering of the world and from which we can learn by use of our minds and consciences.

We learn about this wisdom in five books of the Bible: Job, Psalms, Proverbs, Song of Songs and Ecclesiastes. These are regarded as canonical by Jews and all Christians. There are, in addition, two books of the Apocrypha, the Wisdom of Solomon and Ecclesiasticus, often known as Sirach, that are fully accepted by Roman Catholic and Orthodox Christians but which have a lesser status for Anglicans and in modern translations are placed between the Old Testament and the New. For the first centuries of the Church's existence, the concept of divine wisdom (Hagia Sophia) had great importance in Christian writing and preaching, and major churches, such as the great church built by the Emperor Justinian in the sixth century in Constantinople (today's Istanbul) were dedicated to her.

There are three remarkable features of Sophia. First, wisdom is feminine and thought of as beautiful. Second, wisdom is reflected in the natural laws of the universe, their balance and harmony, and these can be studied with our rational minds. And, third, wisdom can and should guide our decisions and behaviour. Here, for example, is one description:

> For she is a breath of the power of God,
> and a pure emanation of the glory of the Almighty;
> therefore nothing defiled gains entrance into her.
> For she is a reflection of eternal light,
> a spotless mirror of the working of God,
> and an image of his goodness.
> Although she is but one, she can do all things,
> and while remaining in herself, she renews all things;
> in every generation she passes into holy souls
> and makes them friends of God, and prophets;
> for God loves nothing so much as the person who lives
>   with wisdom.
> She is more beautiful than the sun,
> and excels every constellation of the stars.
> Compared with the light she is found to be superior,
> for it is succeeded by the night,
> but against wisdom evil does not prevail.
> She reaches mightily from one end of the earth to the other
> And she orders all things well.
> I loved her and sought her from my youth,
> And I desired to take her for my bride,
> And I became enamoured of her beauty.
> (Wisdom of Solomon 7.25—8.2)

Of these three features, the first – the emphasis on the feminine aspect of the divine – is especially welcome in a tradition where God has been overwhelmingly thought of in male terms. Of course, strictly speaking, there is no gender in God, or rather, all that we think of as masculine and feminine are contained in their fullness and perfection within the divine. As the above quotation makes clear, moreover, the rational order of the universe, which is basic to scientific understanding, has its origin in divine wisdom. The wonderful order and symmetry of nature, its patterns and predictability, which is the foundation of rational thought, reflects divine wisdom. Third, the teaching of Wisdom as we have it in the wisdom literature in the Bible, which has a great deal in common with the ancient wisdom literature of other countries, offers both insights into how the world works, and a prudential guide to living. It sets out ways of behaving that make for the well-being of both those who live in this way and those affected by their actions. It is, as we would say, a consequentialist ethic. It is set out in the form: If you do this, that will follow – so a rational person will be guided by this teaching.

All three of the above aspects of wisdom are important, for they help to correct some misconceptions. They encourage us to see the whole wondrous universe as it is unveiled and explored by science as an expression of divine wisdom. The sheer elegance and beauty of the universe, as noted by our most distinguished mathematicians, draw us to it. And this divine ordering will be reflected in the moral insights of all who think rationally about how to live. So although the Christian faith offers a distinctive view of all goodness and virtue as being ultimately grounded in the being and will of God, it will be possible to find many points of commonality with people of goodwill, whatever religious or cultural background they come from, including our own secular intellectual one.

A prayer used in the Advent season, shortly before Christmas, that in Latin begins '*O Sapientia*' (O Wisdom), gives expression to this theme. The original English version includes the phrase 'the way of prudence', but as this now has a rather different, narrow meaning from its original usage I have substituted the phrase 'how to live wisely and well':

> O Wisdom coming forth from the mouth of the most high,
> Reaching from one end to the other mightily and sweetly
>   ordering all things:
> Come and teach us how to live wisely and well.

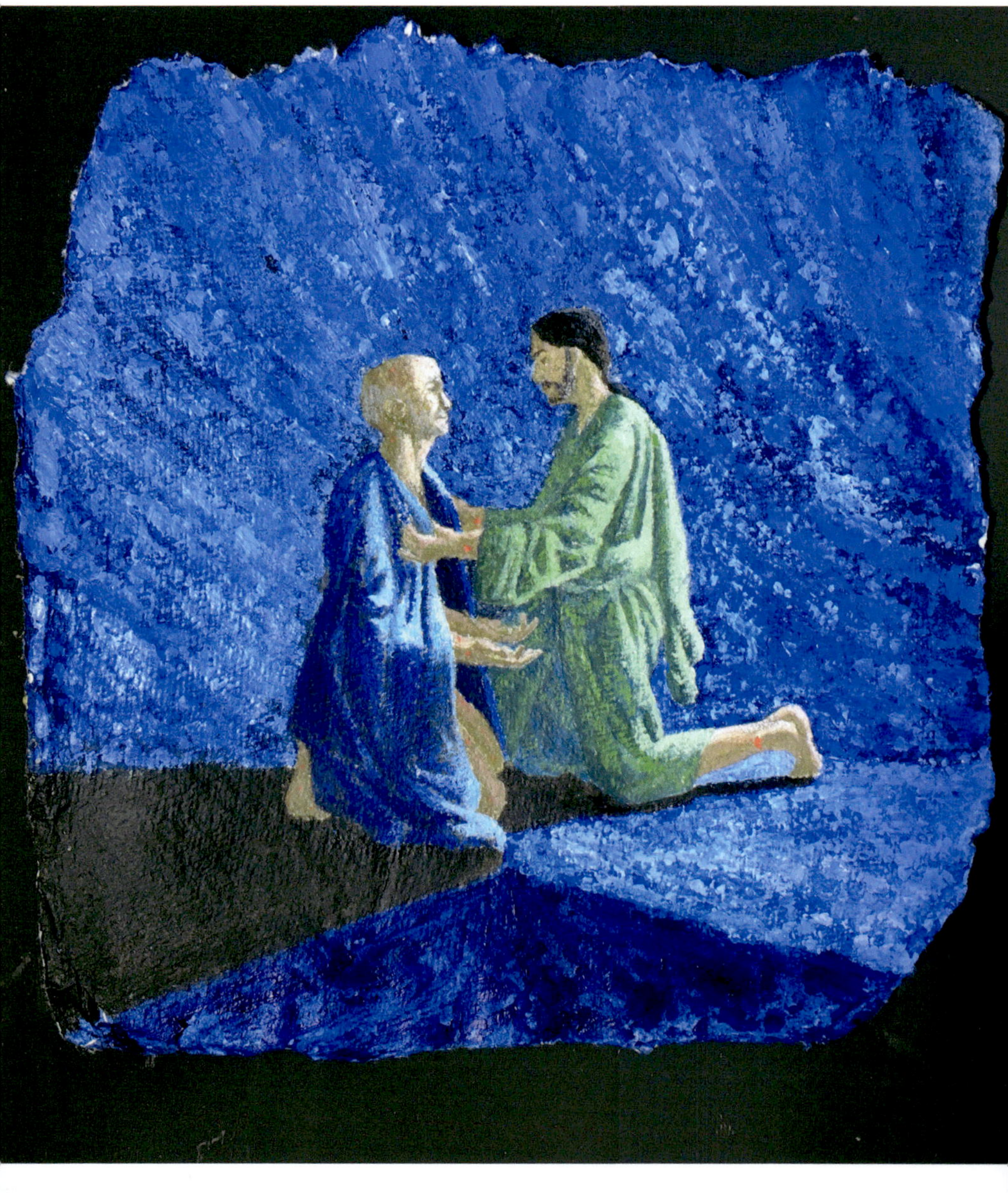

9
Suffering

Roger Wagner, *And the Lord Lifted Up Job's Face*, 1995

The unveiling of the divine mystery in the law, the prophets and the wisdom literature reveals that at the heart of the universe is a wise and loving power. The Hebrew scriptures describe this power as characterized by *hesed*, or loving kindness. But people of the Old Testament period, as now, quickly discovered that much of their experience seemed to contradict this – a contradiction that comes into focus in the book of Job, one of the world's great works of literature.

This painting is one of a series of 13 studies by Roger Wagner (b. 1975) based on the biblical account, and which begin with Job sitting cross-legged, his face in his hands. As the series continues, a figure appears creating the stars, lightning and the wonders of the animal world. Eventually Job acknowledges the mystery and majesty of God:

> But I have spoken of things which I have not understood,
> Things too wonderful for me to know . . .
> I knew you then only by report,
> But now I see you with my own eyes.
> Therefore I yield, repenting in dust and ashes.
> (Job 42.3, 5–6)

This leads on to the final painting in the study, illustrated here, in which God lifts up Job's face. In this painting Job is shown kneeling before another figure. The various brilliant shades of blue create a surreal atmosphere that indicates the dialogue going on in Job's mind as he questions God and God answers him out of the whirlwind. The title *And the Lord Lifted Up Job's Face* is a literal translation of Job 42.9, sometimes translated 'And the Lord showed favour to Job'.

The book of Job contains a prose introduction in which God is shown allowing Job's faith to be tested, and a prose conclusion in which his faithfulness is rewarded. The main poetic body of the work, however, is made up of descriptions of Job's suffering and his protest against the views of his friends as they offer the conventional reasons for his affliction. They try to suggest he is being justly punished for doing wrong, or being tested for the strength of his faith. Job fiercely rejects this received wisdom. He demands to have it out with God himself. In the end, he is given a vision of the grandeur and glory of God's creation – a kind of wildlife film on a large scale – that reduces him to awestruck silence.

People are divided as to whether they find this a satisfactory response to Job's suffering. Certain straightforward points, however, can be made on the subject. First, when God says 'Let there be', he gives creation a life of its own: indeed, to be created is just that – to have a life of one's own, whether as an electron or a cell. This created life operates according to observed regularities on the basis of which we can plan our lives, such as the fact that the sun will rise tomorrow and the law of gravity will still hold. With us humans this autonomous life becomes self-conscious and the regularities in nature make it possible for us to make rational, moral choices. So far as we can understand these things, the world has to be like this if we are to be here as thinking, choosing beings at all.

However, God does not just stand back and watch things go their way. He interacts with every human spirit. Even more than this, in Christ he enters into the flux of human history and suffers the consequences of creating a world in which we do evil to one another.

But, Christians believe, he was raised from the dead and through his spirit lives in our hearts. This is a sign and pledge that in the end, through him, all evil, including death, will be overcome and 'God will be all in all'.

Job did not know this, but he seems to have had some intuition that God's purpose would finally prevail. Words sometimes said at the beginning of a funeral service, and which have been made famous as part of Handel's Messiah, are taken from Job 19.25: 'For I know that my redeemer liveth, and that he shall stand at the latter Day upon the earth' (KJV). Job believes he will be vindicated and that in the end his face will be lifted up to God.

One lesson of Job's story is that we should reject facile solution to the great challenge of suffering and continue to bring our questions and protests to God himself. Certain things can and should be said, as was sketched out with such brevity above, but there is no final resolution of the contradiction in this life between the God of the tsunami and the God who says to us, 'Come unto me all who are weary and heavy laden and I will refresh you' (Matthew 11.28).[5]

In Roger Wagner's Job series, the God who shows the grandeur and terror of creation is a humble Jesus who comes to kneel before us. In the painting reproduced here he is on the same level as Job, lifting his face so that he can look into Job's eyes. For believers, it is this experience of the humble servant God, kneeling at our level, that enables them to live with the contradiction between the love of God known in Christ and the harshness of so much human experience, and to work to reconcile the two by doing what they can to alleviate the suffering of others.[6]

We lift into your presence O God all who suffer in body, mind or spirit, especially those who feel crushed and in despair. May your healing presence and power be with them.

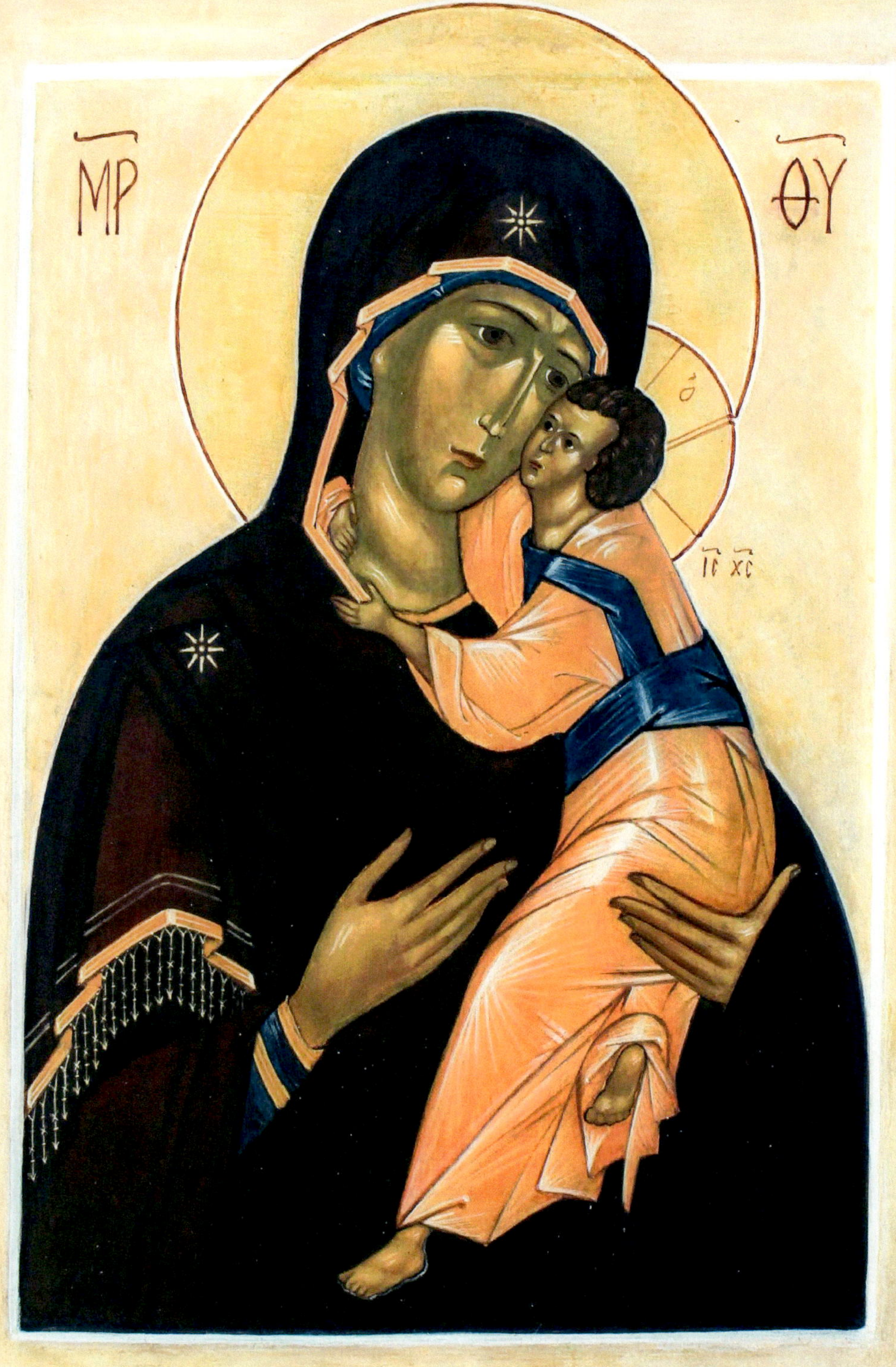

ΜΡ ΘΥ
ΙΣ ΧΣ

10

'The Word became flesh and dwelt among us'

Patricia Fostiropoulos, Icon of loving kindness, 1990

Some Christians might be uneasy about this icon of loving kindness because the artist Patricia Fostiropoulos (b. 1949) makes the figure of Mary so dominant. But the central fact about it – and also for example about another type of icon called the Hodegetria – is that Mary is pointing to the infant Christ. We may be drawn to her beautiful, solemn face, but she then directs our attention away from herself to the babe in her arms.

Many people are still familiar with the Christmas stories, of how three Magi from the East, following a star, came to worship a babe in a crib; of how shepherds saw a vision of angels and were likewise directed to a stable in which there was an infant king to be adored. These wonderful stories are told to bring out a fundamental truth at the heart of the Christian faith – that the eternal Word of God is now to be known in and through a human life. Most importantly, this human life was a divine life from the very beginning. He was not just a good person who had been raised into divinity. He was not just a religiously inspired person. He had been conceived entirely as a result of divine initiative, when an angel appeared to Mary and the Holy Spirit overshadowed her, a truth that the Church celebrates at the Feast of the Annunciation.

On Christmas night every year the amazing prologue to St John's Gospel (John 1.1–14) is read. This passage is about the Eternal Word (*logos*) of God. If its first hearers had been Jews, this would have brought to mind the Word of God that created the universe and spoke through the prophets. If they had been Greeks, they would have thought of the rational principle that runs through the world and which is focused in our human capacity to think and make moral choices. This Word, which is also symbolized as light, is said to enlighten everyone who comes into the world. When the great St Augustine of Hippo in North Africa converted to the Christian faith in 386, at the age of 31, he wrote that all this prologue had been familiar to him in his years as a philosopher and adherent of other religions, except one thing. What he had not met, he said, was the dramatic statement 'And the Word became flesh'.

This is the amazing, beautiful claim at the centre of the Christian faith: 'And the word was made flesh, and dwelt among us, and we beheld his glory, the glory as of the only begotten of the Father, full of grace and truth' (John 1.14, KJV).

Another passage in the New Testament describes how God 'emptied himself' to become human (Philippians 2.1–10, NRSV). While the Eternal Word continues to uphold and animate the whole creation, at the same time he accepts all the limitations of a human life. 'He made himself nothing', as a modern translation puts it. So in this icon we see the Word entirely dependent on his mother, holding on to her and pressing against her cheek, for as is the case with every human child, he needs to receive love through her and be bonded to her, in order to experience the affirmation that is essential for his sense of self-worth. This is an icon in the Russian tradition, where the particular emphasis is on the tenderness of Mary. At the same time there is no sentimentality here, but solemnity, because Mary not only knows that her son will suffer but feels compassion for all suffering creation.

The Christian faith claims that Jesus is at once fully and truly divine and fully and truly human, while remaining one true and proper person. We cannot fully understand this mystery, but in order to get even a glimpse of its truth we need to remember that God is not another *thing*. He does not compete with our space as though the more of him there is, the less there is of us. On the contrary, the more God fills us, the more fully and truly we are ourselves. That filling by God was so complete in the case of Jesus that we have to talk of a personal identity. Having said that, there is a further difference between Jesus and any other human life. As one great Christian thinker, Austin Farrer, wrote:

> The very action of Jesus is divine action – It is what God does about the salvation of the world. In the common case of a good human life, humanity supplies the pattern and God the grace. In Jesus, divine redemptive action supplies the pattern, and manhood the medium or instrument. A good man helped by Grace may do human things divinely. Christ did divine things humanly.[7]

In doing divine things humanly, God limited himself. He accepted all the constraints of being human. But this limitation, as the poet Richard Crashaw (1613–49) puts it, is to lift our lives to heaven:

> Welcome all wonders in one sight,
> Eternity shut in a span,
> Summer in Winter, day in night,
> Heaven in earth, and God in man,
> Great little one, whose all embracing birth
> Lifts earth to heaven, stoops heaven to earth.

So we could pray:

> Jesus, Eternal Word of the Father,
> You shared our humanity.
> May we so live in your love
> That we come to share your divinity.

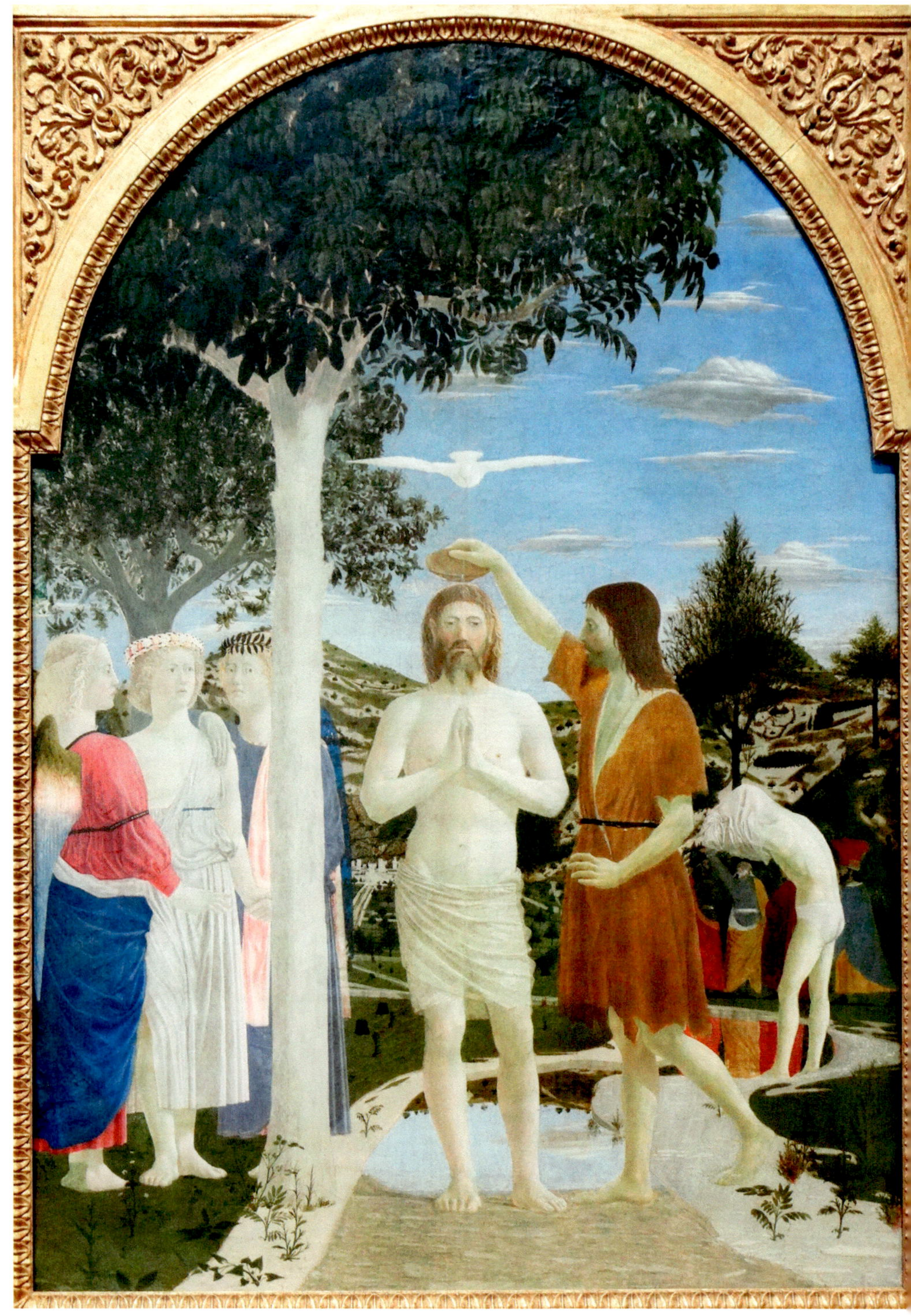

11

The baptism of Christ

Piero della Francesca, *The Baptism of Christ, c.* 1450

Not surprisingly, the baptism of Christ has been depicted since the earliest days of Christian art. This representation by Piero della Francesca (1416–92) was painted for the priory of St John the Baptist at Sansepolcro, in Tuscany, where he lived. There may be a glimpse of the town in the painting, with the baptism staged against the background of some very characteristic Italian landscape. The artist follows traditional iconography, but engages perspective in the style of the early Renaissance, and includes his own contemporaries as onlookers at the baptism.

In classical understanding the marks of beauty were balance, symmetry, wholeness, harmony and radiance. All are present here. There is a strong horizontal emphasis, with the dove flattened to match the clouds, and an equally strong vertical one with the trees and standing figures. But this sharp contrast is softened by the curve of the figure undressing behind John the Baptist, and by the Baptist's lifted leg. At the same time a luminous light picks out the white of the bodies, the bark of the tree and sunlit fields in contrast to the dark of the leaves. All is momentarily still in the light of revelation. It is that luminous stillness which the painting captures so well.

The Gospel accounts (Matthew 3.13–17; Mark 1.9–11; Luke 3.21–3) describe how Christ hears a heavenly voice: 'This is my beloved Son in whom I am well pleased', with the Holy Spirit, symbolized as a dove, descending upon him. The people of Israel were called to live as a son in relation to God ('Out of Egypt have I called my son', Hosea 11.1). This vocation of sonship becomes focused in Jesus, who through God's Spirit dwelling within him lived out his whole life faithfully in relation to the one he addressed as 'Abba, Father'.

People understandably puzzle away at what might be meant by addressing God as Father, Son and Holy Spirit, but the basis for this is Jesus' actual life. Jesus lived as a Son in relation to the Father, through the power of the Holy Spirit. This is the life of God made accessible in human terms. Moreover, it is a life in which Christians partake, for all Christians are baptized 'In the name of the Father and the Son and the Holy Spirit'. We are taken into that life and called to make it manifest as we live as daughters or sons in relation to our heavenly Father, and are enabled to do so through his indwelling and empowering spirit.

Some people were baptized as adults, and they remember the event vividly. Many more were baptized as children; though they cannot remember it, the meaning is the same. As the great reformer Martin Luther, who was baptized as an infant, used to remind himself, '*Baptizatus sum*, I have been baptized.' One of the advances of the ecumenical movement is that, though the churches are still divided on a number of matters, they accept the validity of the baptism of all those baptized in the name of the Father and the Son and the Holy Spirit. Through this faith and baptism we are not only daughters and sons of God but sisters and brothers to one another. We are 'in Christ', and this means that the words that rang in the ears of Jesus can ring in our ears also. 'This is my beloved, in whom I am well pleased.'

O God, Father, holding me in being.
O God Eternal Son, enfolding me with your love.
O God, Holy Spirit, filling me with your life.
God beyond me, God beside me, God within me,
Father, Son and Spirit,
ever to be worshipped and adored.

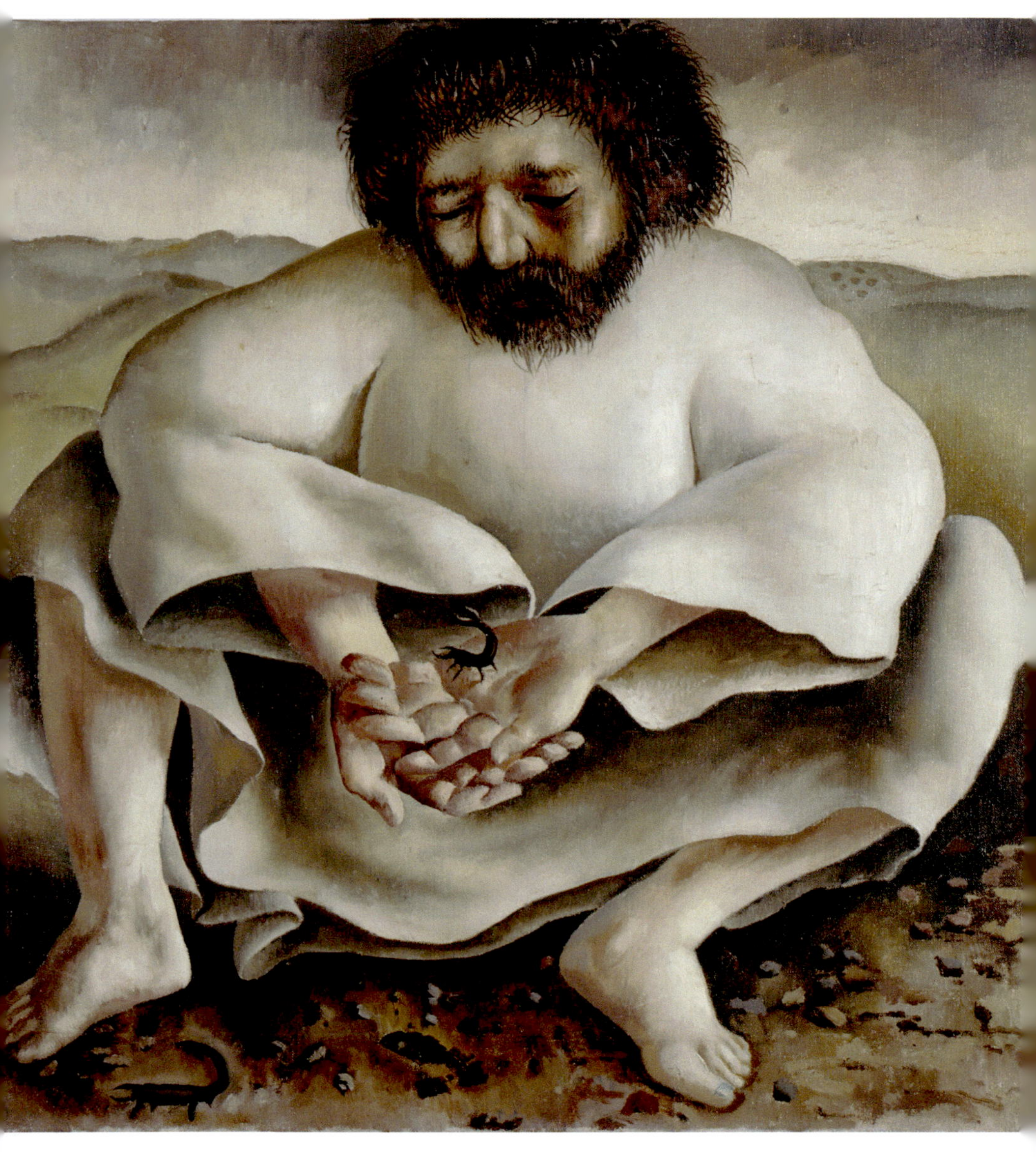

12
The testing of Christ
Stanley Spencer, *The Scorpion*, 1939

After Jesus was baptized, Mark records that he was driven by the spirit into the wilderness for 40 days to be tempted by Satan, and that there he found himself among the wild beasts (Mark 1.12–13). Stanley Spencer (1891–1951) produced a series of paintings of Christ in the wilderness, of which this is one. What is particularly moving here is the way Christ is looking down at the scorpion in his hand.

At his baptism Jesus was assured that he was indeed the Son of God. But how was he to use this status? How was his sonship to be lived out?

Alone in the desert, Jesus became vividly aware of three mistaken ways in which he could do this: three temptations or tests, each one preceded by the phrase '*If* you are the Son of God . . .'. He was tempted to satisfy his personal needs by turning stones into bread; to gain followers by performing dramatic stunts; and to use evil means to achieve good ends.

It is easy to slip into thinking that if Jesus was the Son of God, his temptations were not severe. On the contrary, just because he was the Son of God, they were more testing than anything we can experience or imagine. They went to the very heart of his vocation and set the course for his whole life. Being the Son of God meant living his life in trustful obedience to his father, whatever the future might bring, and as his ministry developed that future looked increasingly threatening and dark.

This period in the wilderness lasted 40 days, a recapitulation of the testing of the people of Israel in the wilderness for 40 years. But the testing did not end there. Luke (4.1–13) gives the temptations in a different order from Matthew (4.1–11). Luke ends them with Jesus imagining how he might throw himself off the Temple parapet, letting God's angels take care of him. He resists this, and then we read: 'The devil departed, biding his time.' That final test, when it came about, entailed blood and agony, when on the cross Jesus was taunted with the same challenge he heard in the desert: '*If* you are the Son of God . . .'. If you are the Son of God, show us by coming down from the cross. But again he resisted this temptation. It was his Father's will that he go through with it to the bitter end; and he was called to trust that good purpose.

Jesus had once likened God to a good father, putting the question: 'If we ask a father for bread, will he give us a scorpion?' But in Stanley Spencer's painting it is just such a scorpion that Jesus cups in his hand, looking down at it with a sense of deep pity. Scorpions can sting us to death, and the painting depicts more scorpions all around Jesus on the ground. It seems as though Jesus is contemplating his future and facing up to his destiny. It will not be bread that his Father gives him, but the sting of death.

Perhaps there is another idea here as well. We humans are like scorpions, stinging one another to death. Despite this, Jesus looks upon us with indescribable pity, a pity that was to take active form in dying to save us from such mutual destruction. As the great English mystic Julian of Norwich (1342–1416) put it, he looks on us 'with pity and not with blame'.

Jesus, friend and brother,
You were tested and found faithful,
When we are tested give us the insight to recognize what is right,
the will to do it,
and strength to continue in the true path.

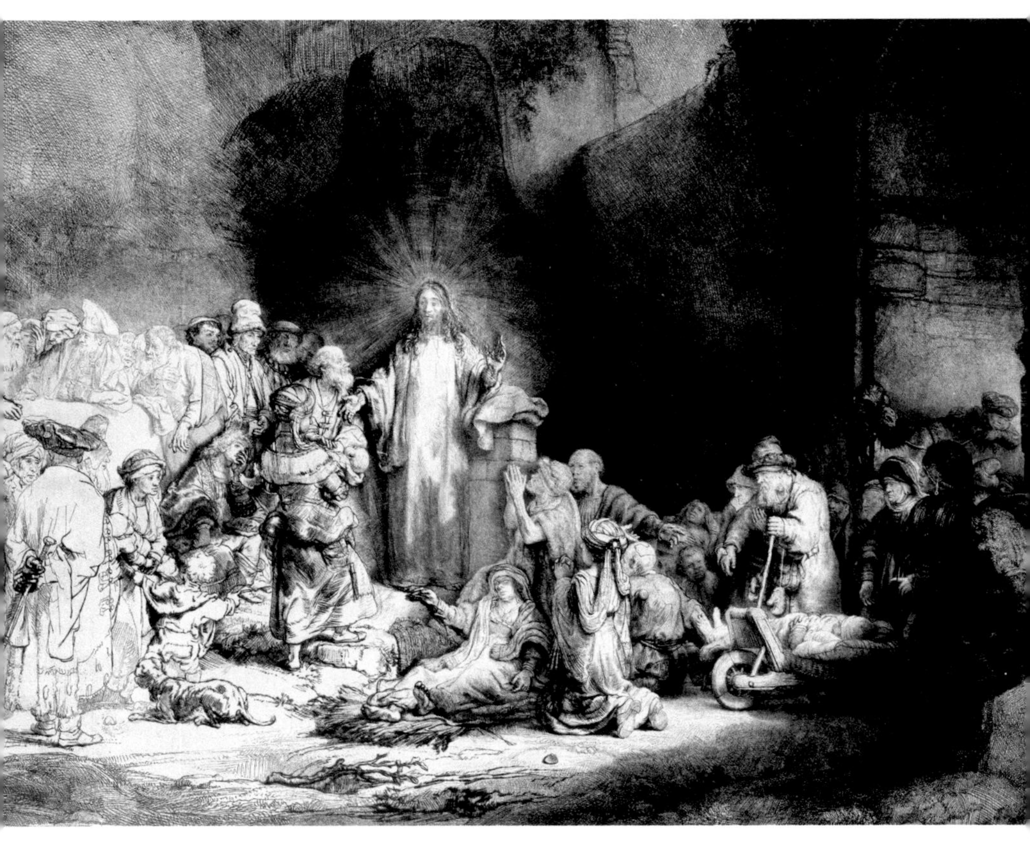

13

The One who knows our needs

Rembrandt, *Christ Healing and Preaching,* *c.* 1648

In the early stages of his life, Rembrandt (1606–69) produced grandiose paintings full of flamboyance. After a period of great anguish, including deaths in his immediate family and imprisonment for debt, his style changed, showing great sensitivity to human suffering. Many of his numerous paintings on biblical themes, like this one, reflect this humility and openness to human pain.

Christ is shown here healing the sick, teaching, and blessing the children brought to him. People look to him and hold out their arms in need. He stands as a bright light in the surrounding darkness. The scene is roughly based on incidents in Matthew chapter 19. Known as the 100 guilder print, it was for a time the most iconic of all Christian images.

Stories of Christ healing people in body and mind account for large sections of the Gospels. We know some people appear to have such a gift of healing. It is not difficult to believe that in Jesus, a man fully at one with God, such a gift should be highly developed. He resisted moves to make him a full-time healer, but it is clear that out of compassion he responded to individual need as far as he could.

Very many people of all religions and none have hugely admired Jesus' teaching, especially as it is set out in the Sermon on the Mount in Matthew 5—7. Here he teaches us that we are to love our enemies and not just our friends, that we are to examine the motives for our actions and look to God, not other people, for approval. We are not to judge or insult others. We are to look at our thoughts and not just our actions. He shows particular concern for the humble and meek, those who lose out in the world as it is now, promising better things in God's kingdom. All the time he lived in total trust in his heavenly Father. Even the hairs of your head are numbered, he said.

There was something hugely attractive both about Jesus' person and his message. It was said that 'the common people heard him gladly' (Mark 12.37). His obvious compassion and his belief that religion was there to help, not oppress us, drew people to him. He refers to a yoke, which was used to carry heavy loads, in the words:

Come to me, all who are weary and whose load is heavy; I will give you rest. Take my yoke upon you, and learn from me, for I am gentle and humble hearted; and you will find rest for your souls. For my yoke is easy to wear, my load is light.
(Matthew 11.28–30)

Many people say they admire Jesus as a great teacher. Jesus, however, made it quite clear, especially to the religious, that what mattered was to act on what he said. Christians, moreover, have always seen in Jesus more than a teacher. The compassion he showed in his ministry is nothing less than a revelation of the compassion God shows for every human being. In him the very heart of God is open and available in human terms. His first followers did not see this immediately, but in the light of his resurrection his life and death were understood to have an eternal significance. It was not only a human life lived for others, but a disclosure of the divine life lived for the world.

As human beings we all have needs of various kinds, physical, emotional and spiritual. We are all needy. We can bring those needs to Christ, for he knows them even before we ask him to help us. Many years ago, when I was at college, a fellow student said to me, 'Our needs are angels.' They open a way for God to get through to us. Those needs are not always met in the way we want, but a way forward may be shown us. Perhaps, for example, a friend is feeling rather sorry for herself. Then some words of a great prayer by St Ignatius come to her mind: 'Teach us not so much to be consoled as to console.' This impels her to go to someone she knows who has recently been bereaved, and the meeting turns out to be mutually enriching.

> Jesus, you know my needs even before I speak.
> I bring them into your healing presence.
> Make me sensitive to the needs of others so that I may bring
> that same healing presence and power into their lives.

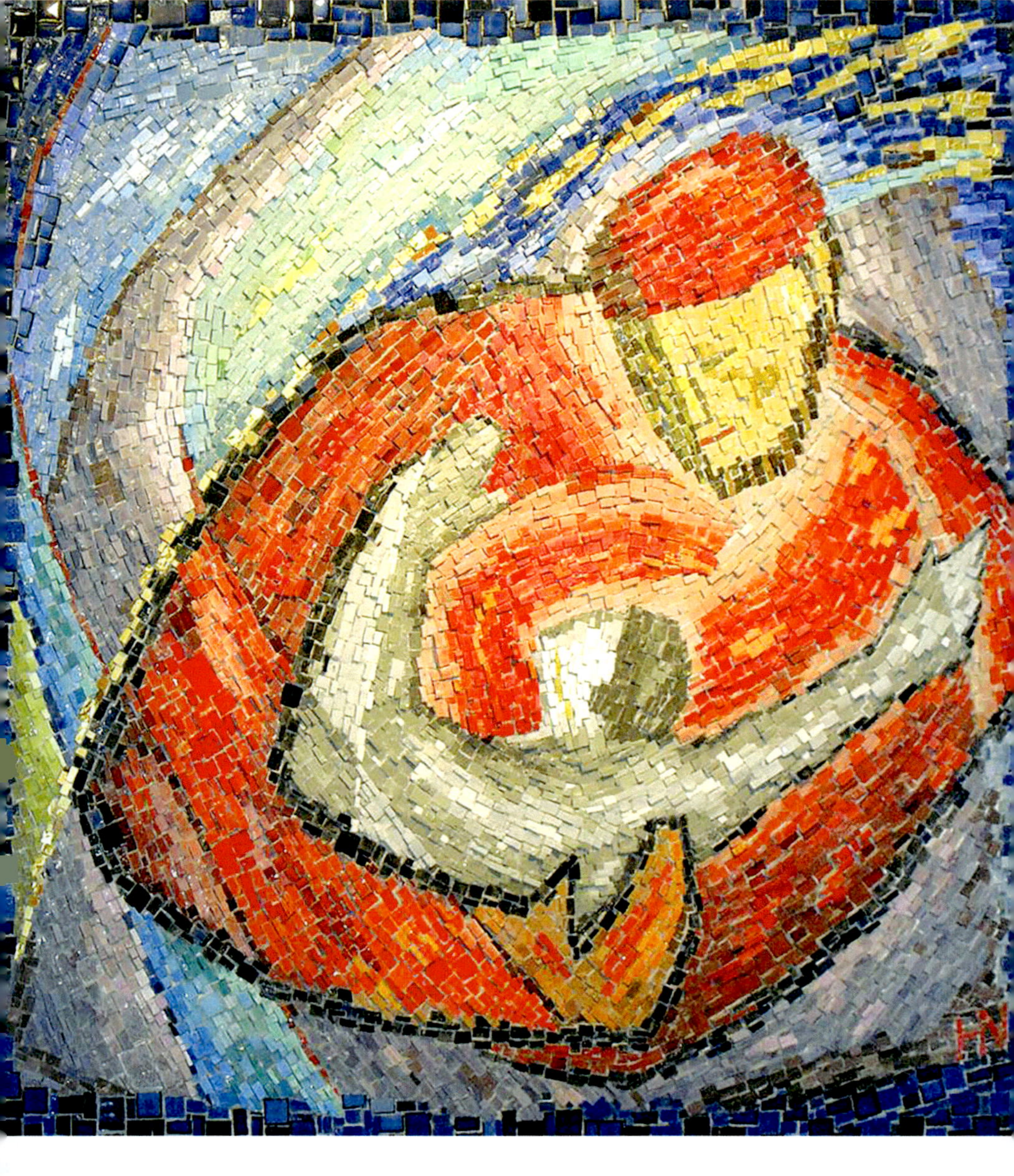

14

Welcomed home

Hildegart Nicholas, *The Prodigal*, 1991

This mosaic is based on what is for many the best loved of all the stories told by Jesus. It tells of a young man who manages to persuade his father to give him his inheritance in advance. He then goes abroad and spends it on high living. Finding himself destitute, he has to take a job feeding pigs. Then, coming to his senses, he realizes he would be better off working for his father than where he is, so he decides to return home and say sorry. Even before he arrives, however, his father is scanning the horizon, and he welcomes him home literally with open arms.

There, for many people, the story ends. In fact, however, there is a further twist. The young man's elder brother, hearing the sounds of the welcoming party, becomes resentful that, although he has worked faithfully for his father over many years, he has never had such a celebration. The father, however, says to him, 'My boy you are always with me, and everything I have is yours. How could we not celebrate this happy day? Your brother here was dead and has come back to life: he was lost and has been found' (Luke 15.11–32).

This story has an important place in the ministry of Jesus. We know he went out of his way to include those whom others excluded, those on the margins of respectable society. He was criticized for this, and it is in response to such criticism that he told this story. His critics are clearly meant to see their behaviour as similar to that of the elder brother.

This ministry of inclusion was vividly taught through other images as well. God is like a shepherd who searches the hills for the one lost sheep, or the woman who scours the floor looking for the one lost coin (Luke 15.1–10). Jesus is saying that what he is doing, including outsiders in the kingdom, is what God does. This is the pattern of God's relationship with us.

Rembrandt painted the most famous representation of this scene, which can be found in the Hermitage, in St Petersburg. It shows the prodigal son kneeling before his father, with the father's hands around his back. People have noticed that one of the hands looks like a man's and one like a woman's, and hence it has been noted that God is a father who loves like a mother. In this mosaic by Hildegart Nicholas (1913–95), however, the focus is not on the earthly ministry of Jesus but on God's eternal embrace of those who turn to him. There is a wonderful, swirling circle of love in which the son is enclosed. All humanity is fully embraced. Jesus' inclusion of those he met is simply an acting out in human terms of the eternal attitude of God towards all his children.

That love embraces us whether we identify with the prodigal or his elder brother. And we are called to live with the same attitude of inclusion. As an old rhyme puts it:

He drew a circle that shut me out
Heretic, rebel, a thing to flout.
Love and I had the wit to win.
We drew a circle that took him in.

Our prayer then might be:

Jesus, as you include me in your embrace, help me to include others.

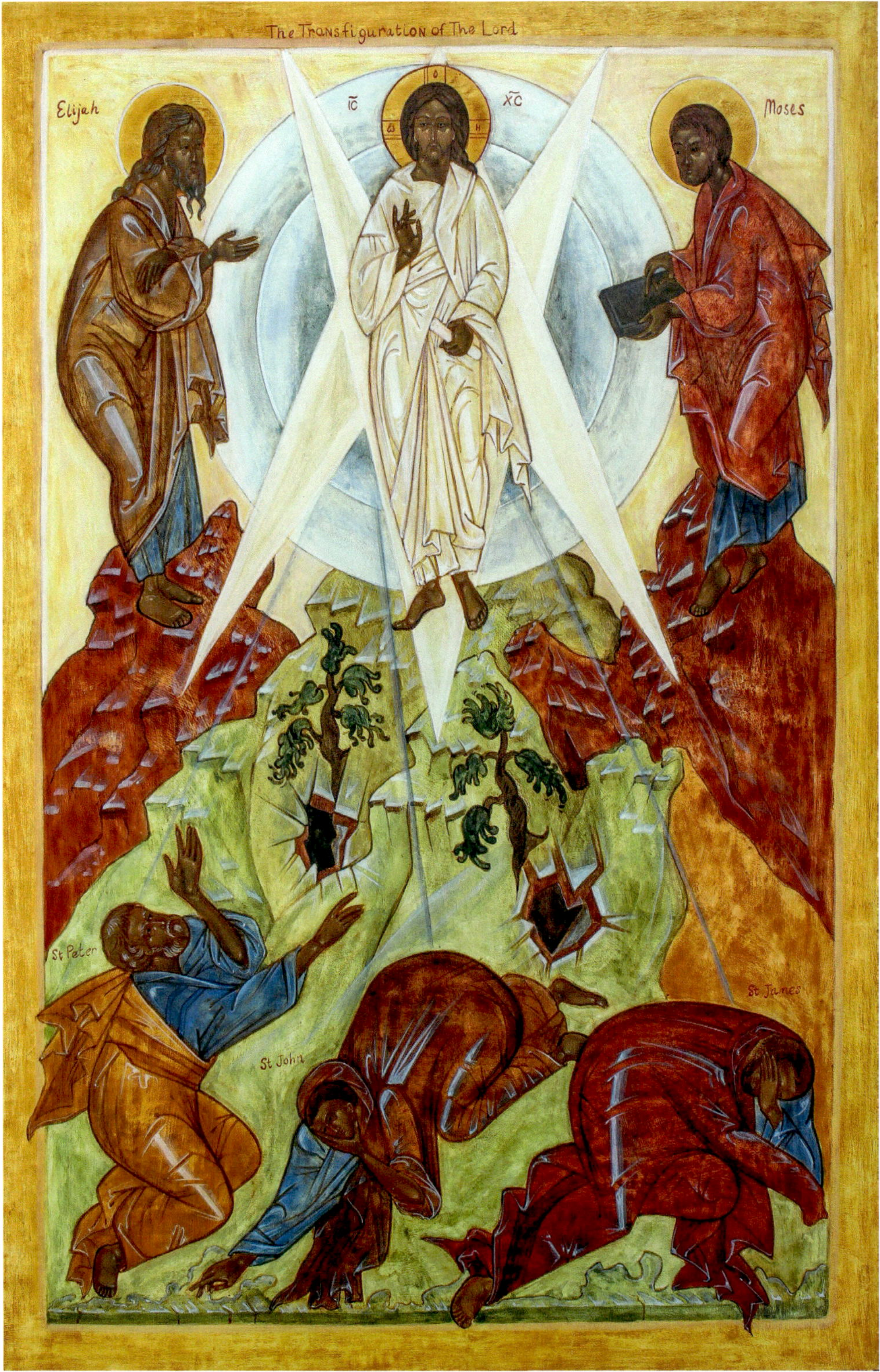

The Transfiguration of The Lord
Elijah
Moses
ΙC ΧC
St Peter
St James
St John

15

'From glory to glory'

Edith Reyntiens, Icon of the Transfiguration after the prototype of Theophanes the Greek,[8] c. 1986

A man was sitting by a hospital bed talking to the patient. What did he see? A frail body emaciated by crippling illness? Yes. A face hollowed by long years of suffering? Yes. Then the patient smiled and began talking quietly. In a moment of transfiguration the visitor saw not so much a body or a face but a person; a person radiating serenity and love. This serenity and love welled up from some deep radiance within, from a heart rooted in God.

Peter, James and John, three close followers of Jesus, once had a similar experience. It was Jesus' custom to go to a quiet place to pray, but on this occasion he took the three with him, right up into the mountains. There they saw him transfigured before their eyes. The earliest account of this incident (Mark 9.2–8) says in a homely image that his robes became dazzling white 'such as no one on earth could bleach them'. In this icon, painted in traditional style by the modern icon painter Edith Reyntiens, the artist goes beyond dazzling white clothes. Jesus appears on a white star, behind which is a mandorla (meaning almond), or aureole of light, made up of concentric circles in varying shades of blue. This was a way of indicating the divinity of Jesus.

In this moment of transfiguration Jesus is not alone. He appears in the icon with Moses on his left and Elijah on his right; Moses with a book in his hand representing the law for living that God gave to his people, Elijah representing the prophets' critique of their failure to live up to God's law. These two disclosures of God's purpose were discussed in earlier reflections. The three disciples also hear a voice saying, 'This is my beloved Son, listen to him.' The law and the prophets point to the fulfilment of God's purpose in Jesus. It is only a momentary vision but it terrifies them, and in the icon we see them turning away, sprawled on the ground.

In Jesus we learn about God. We also learn about ourselves. We learn who we really are, our true vocation and destiny. The early Christians were fond of saying that God became what we are in order that we might become as he is. We learn that Jesus is the Son of God revealed in human terms. We also learn that, through him, this is just what we are called to become, daughters or sons of God.

In the story of the transfiguration, and through this icon, we also learn that Jesus' sonship is resplendent with glory. The disciples saw it in Jesus, but through him it is intended for us too. In a fine passage St Paul wrote that we, beholding the glory of the Lord, 'are being transformed into the same image from glory to glory' (2 Corinthians 3.18). In the light of the good news provided by their faith, Christians discover something of that glory in themselves.

For it is the God who said, 'Let light shine out of darkness who has shone in our hearts to give the light of the knowledge of the glory of God in the face of Jesus Christ'.
(2 Corinthians 4.6)

When things are going badly for us, or when we look at the world and find it in a terrible state, it is easy to lose heart. It is perhaps particularly easy for those suffering from long-term illness, whether physical or mental, to do so. But all the time, according to St Paul, something can be happening within us.

So we do not lose heart. Even though our outer nature is wasting away, our inner nature is being renewed day by day. For

this slight momentary affliction is preparing us for an eternal weight of glory beyond all measure, because we look not at what can be seen but at what cannot be seen; for what can be seen is temporary, but what cannot be seen is eternal.
(2 Corinthians 4.16–18)

In our earthly life this is for the most part a hidden glory. During his ministry, for example, few people saw it in Jesus. It was only after his resurrection that the first Christians really grasped the truth that is in him. As St Paul said, the rulers of this age did not understand, 'for if they had they would not have crucified the Lord of glory' (1 Corinthians 2.8). So it is that we too can all too easily dismiss or ignore or write off other people, and miss the glory that is in them.

Risen, ascended, glorified Lord, open our eyes to see something of your glory in the people we meet day by day, and so live in us that they may see something of your glory in us.

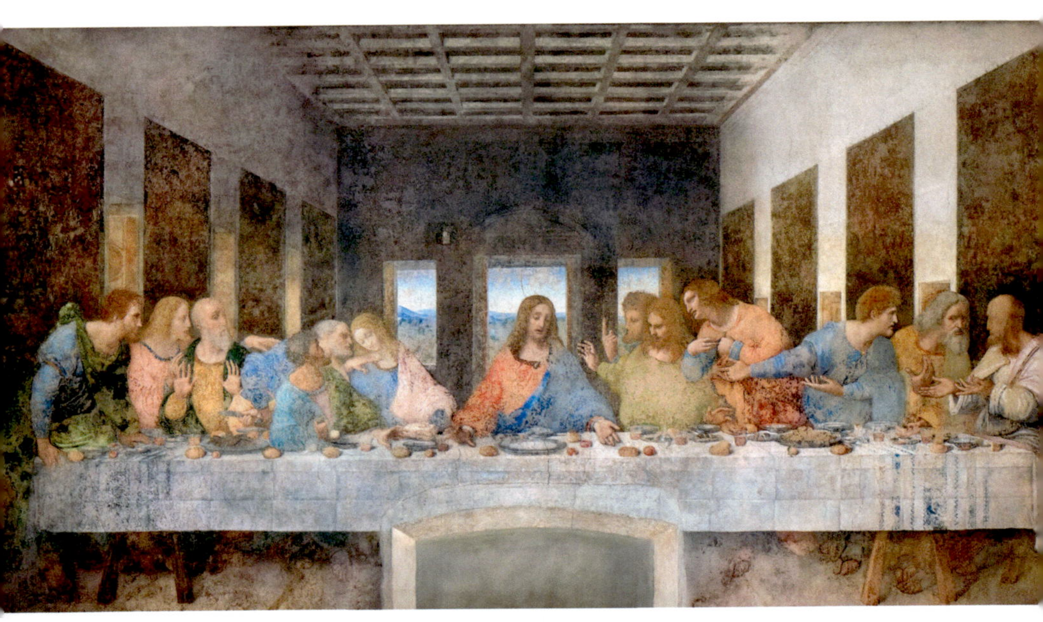

16

The Last Supper

Leonardo da Vinci, *The Last Supper*, 1494–98

One vacation when I was a student I went camping with a group of friends on the continent, where we visited as many museums, galleries and churches as we could. As I stood in the convent of Santa Maria delle Grazie in Milan before Leonardo da Vinci's (1452–1519) famous representation of the Last Supper, I was overwhelmed and silent. It was as though I was in the room with the disciples. The painting takes up the whole wall of the convent's refectory; over the years it had deteriorated very badly but by 1999, after 21 years' work, it had been restored (there is a good copy of it by Giampietrino in the Royal Academy in London). Leonardo has captured the moment when Christ announces that one of those present will betray him. They are all in a state of consternation, as expressed in the gestures of their arms and hands, asking who on earth it can possibly be.

From the first days of the Church it has been the custom of Christians to meet for a shared meal of a special kind. These gatherings are variously called the Mass, the Liturgy, Holy Communion, the Lord's Supper or the Eucharist, the Greek word for thanksgiving. Christians have done this because of what Jesus told them to do at the last meal he had with them. The earliest account we have of this last supper is from a letter of St Paul written about the year AD 53:

> For the tradition which I handed on to you came from the Lord himself: that on the night of his arrest the Lord Jesus took bread and after giving thanks to God broke it and said, 'This is my body, which is for you; do this in memory of me.' In the same

way, he took the cup after supper, and said: 'This cup is the new covenant sealed by my blood. Whenever you drink it, do this in memory of me.' For every time you eat this bread and drink this cup, you proclaim the death of the Lord, until he comes. (1 Corinthians 11.23–26)

Jesus was first of all looking to his anticipated death on the following day and wanting his disciples to understand that this was not a tragic waste but a life given for them. The broken body and poured-out blood were for the world's salvation.

Second, he was saying that after his death he wanted his followers to hold a special meal together in his memory, in which the bread and wine would become vehicles for his continuing presence among them. Since the sixteenth century there have, sadly, been fierce disagreements between Christians about the sense in which we receive Christ in the Eucharist. Whatever the differences, however, all Christians believe he is present with them. None believe he is absent! Furthermore, there is now much greater agreement on this issue than there has been for five centuries. The emphasis now is on Christ being present in the whole eucharistic gathering – the readings from Scripture, the preaching, the prayers of the faithful, the taking, blessing, breaking and receiving of the bread. Some wise words attributed to Queen Elizabeth I remain applicable today:

'Twas Christ the Word that spake it.
I took the bread and brake it.
And what the Word did make it,
that I believe and take it.

Some people today, understandably, find the language of the Eucharist too stark and shocking, with its imagery of eating Christ's body and drinking his blood. It is indeed stark and shocking. What this language is meant to convey, however, is nothing less than our total transformation, our becoming the body of Christ in the world by taking his body into ourselves. It is said that we are what we eat. We eat Christ, spiritually and sacramentally, in order to be formed into his likeness. We receive Christ in order to become his presence in the world. A well-known prayer in most Anglican liturgies asks that we may so receive the body and blood of Christ that 'he may dwell in us and we in him'.

Christ is recorded as saying: 'I am the bread of Life.' In a long passage reflecting on these words, he goes on to say that we have to eat this bread, for it is essential both now and for ever (John 6). It is this bread that sustains and nourishes our whole Christian life, spiritually and sacramentally.

A sacrament is defined as something outward and visible with an inward and spiritual meaning. The whole world is a sacrament in this sense, for we live in a material universe and matter has been created good. 'Earth's crammed with heaven, and every common bush afire with God', as Elizabeth Barrett Browning put it. There are, however, two special biblical sacraments: baptism and the Eucharist. Through confessing faith in Christ and baptism by water in the name of the Father, the Son and the Holy Spirit we become incorporated in Christ. Through the bread and wine we receive in the eucharistic community we are fed with his life. Christ told us to do this. It is a very simple thing to do. Some would say that gathering with other Christians on the Lord's Day to do just this is the bare minimum of a Christian way of life.

Jesus, you are the bread of life.
Feed us with yourself that we may be a sign of your presence
in the world.

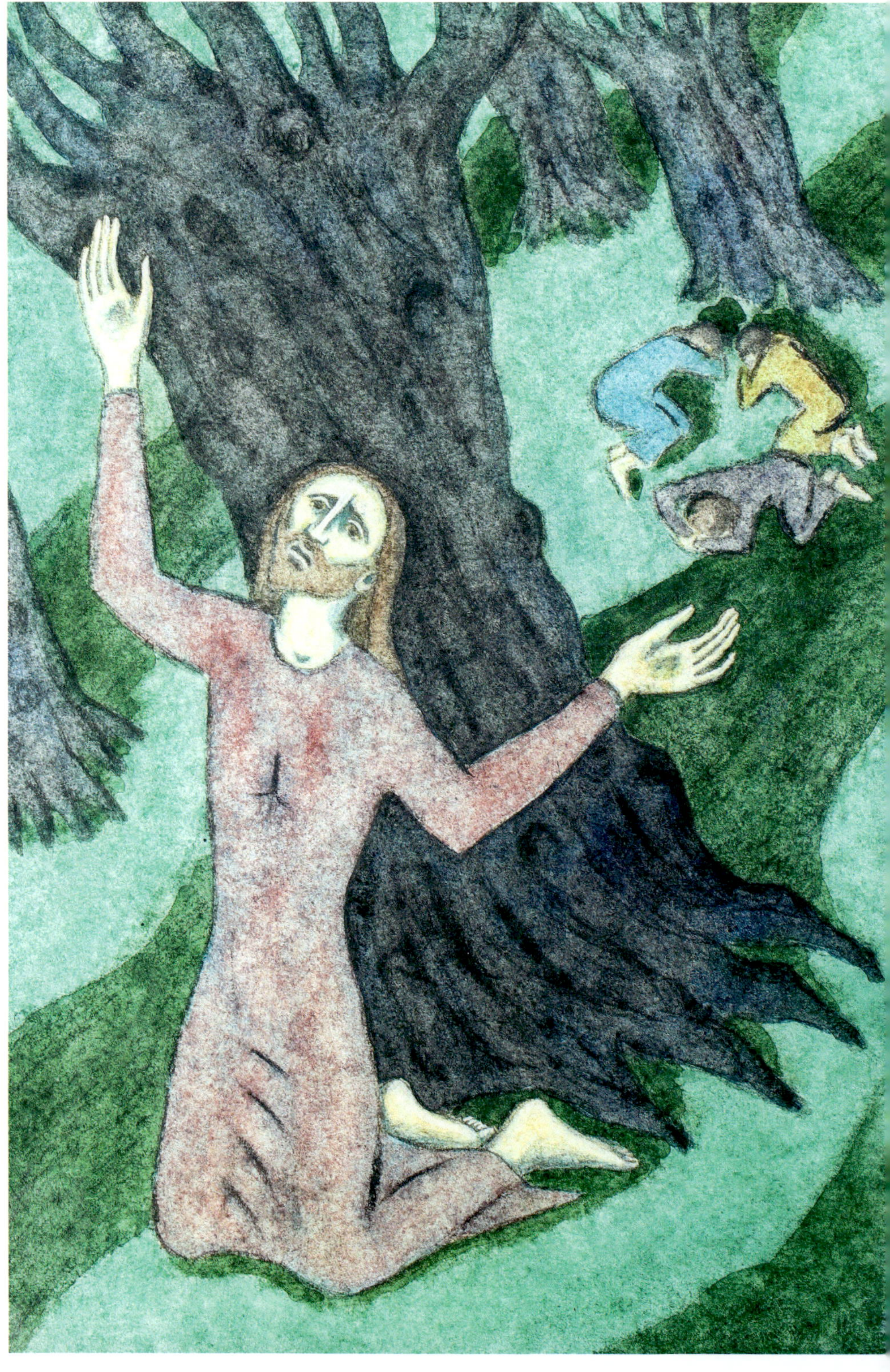

17
Agony

Helen Meyer, *Agony in the Garden of Gethsemane, c.* 1990

In this painting by Helen Meyer (b. 1929), Jesus kneels, face open and turned upwards, praying in deep anguish in the garden of Gethsemane. In traditional representations of this scene, based on Mark 14.32–42, the perspective is that of the three apostles, Peter, James and John, looking towards Jesus who prays a little way from them. Here the perspective is from before the face of Jesus, looking down the slope to where the three apostles seem curled up in sleep. The ancient olive trees with their stark branches and roots, like so many claws, together with the incised bark, create a sense of menace heightened by the dark shadows they cast over the whole scene. The light (from the moon?) picks out the face, hands and feet of Jesus, each hand with a dark patch in it, as though anticipating the nails.

Jesus was not a suicide. Like any human being he had a strong will to live. But he recognized early in his ministry that he was arousing opposition. He knew that if he took his message to the spiritual and political centre of the country, opposition from vested interests would intensify and lead to his rejection – and worse. But he knew that this was where he had to go. This painting depicts the scene, recounted in all four Gospels and referred to in two other passages in the New Testament, when the tension between Jesus's will to live and his sense of vocation reached its climax. Jesus went into the ancient olive grove of Gethsemane (the name probably means 'olive-press'), on the lower slopes of the Mount of Olives facing Jerusalem, to pray.

He did not want to die and he may also have been conscious of some dense spiritual darkness he would have to endure through entering into our human estrangement from God. So he prayed desperately that he might not have to go through with it. 'Horror and anguish overwhelmed him and he said "My heart is ready to break with grief"' (Mark 14.33–34). He then pleaded with his heavenly Father to take the cup of suffering from him. He prayed this not once but three times. So great was the agony that according to one account his sweat, like great drops of blood, fell to the ground (Luke 22.44). But Jesus added, 'Not my will but thine be done.' And this meant that he could not back down. He had to go on, and this resulted in his crucifixion the next day.

In ordinary human life we often resent carrying out someone else's will, particularly if that person has power and we do not. Their will comes across as a threat to our will: the more there is of them, the less there is of us. But God is not an object in the world of objects. His will is not a will in the world of wills, to limit or threaten our will. His will is the wellspring from which our being flows, the good purpose in which our will finds its repose and poise. It is not a threat, except in our imagination, but is where we find our peace and meaning. This is the very heart of the Christian life: seeking the will of God for our life as a whole and all the details within it. This will is a will of love, which desires our growth into all that we have within us to be. It is not alien to us but is the deepest core of our being.

Gracious God,
Your kingdom come.
Your will be done,
in me and through me.

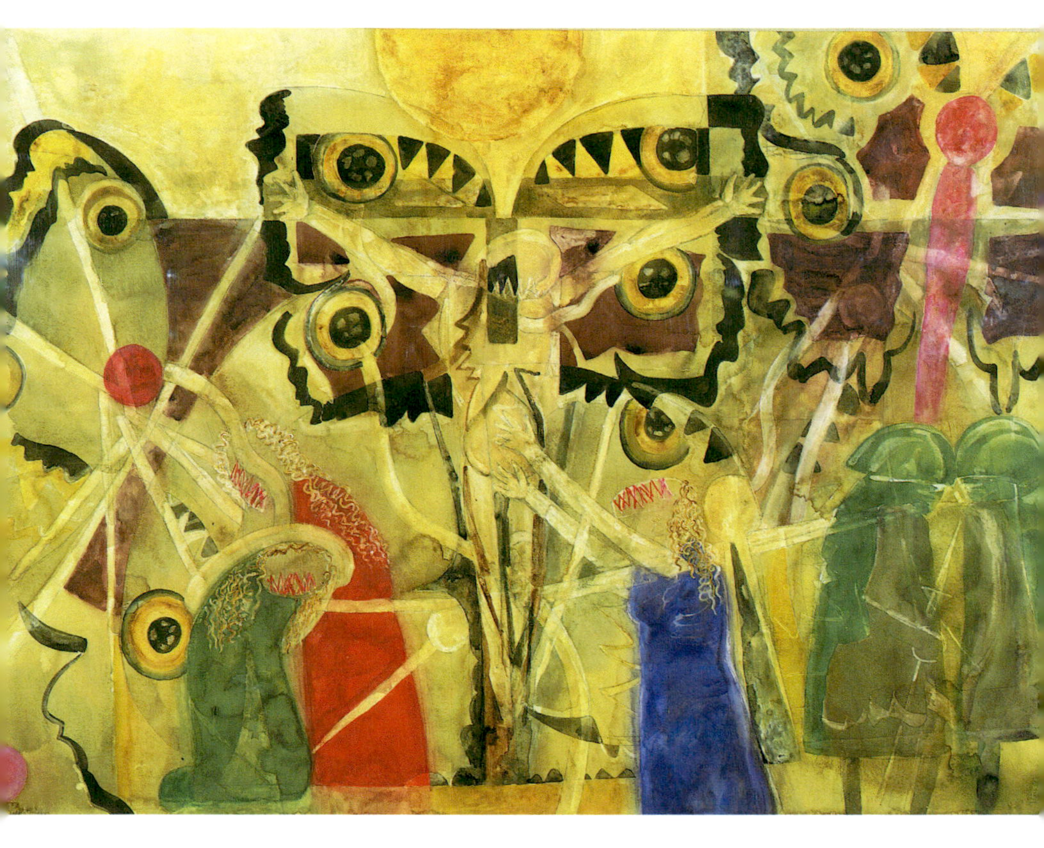

18

Crucified and risen

Norman Adams, *The Golden Crucifixion*, 1993

In the centre of this painting by Norman Adams (1927–2005), Christ is on the cross, arms outstretched. As we look, however, we can begin to make out other figures. Some are clearly grieving: two figures stand, one in blue reaching out, one in red on the other side looking away; one in green is kneeling. To the right of these figures are two soldiers in green, who, together with the patches of black in the picture, exude a sense of menace. But the painting is dominated not by the cross but by a pair of fabulous butterfly wings.

The cross is to be seen in the light of the resurrection. For the resurrection was not so much a reversal of the cross as a revelation of its true meaning. It revealed that Christ, even when he might have been emotionally distraught, was perfectly at one with his heavenly Father. In him, God and humanity, heaven and earth, were joined, never to be unjoined. That relationship was not destroyed at death but revealed as eternal, and through the cross Christians are united with Christ and taken into that relation.

Central to the Christian message is the belief that Christ came to bring about our salvation. But what is this salvation? It is, quite simply, living with trust and love towards our good Creator; being at one with the ground of our being. The word atonement is sometimes used of the means that brings this about. The word breaks down into *at-one-ment*.

This implies of course that such unity is presently lacking. We only have to hear or read the news for a few moments to know that, collectively, humanity is estranged or alienated from the good purpose of our Creator. His purpose is that we should love him and one

81

another. But we do not do this, and a breach has opened up between God and humanity. Christ came to overcome that breach. When humans quarrel, someone has to take the initiative to make it up and someone has to say sorry. God has taken the initiative by coming among us in Christ and inviting us into his kingdom.

God does not need to be appeased before he forgives us. His willingness to forgive always stands ready. In Jesus' famous parable of the prodigal son discussed earlier, the father scans the horizon looking for his son and welcomes him home with open arms. It is the son who comes to his senses and says sorry (Luke 15.11–32).

Forgiveness is not so much about wiping the slate clean as continuing to hold someone in relationship even though that person has hurt you. God continues to hold us in relationship, and the cross is an indication of the hurt we do to him. He came among us to embrace us, and we killed him. This puts a huge question mark against every estimate we make of ourselves and our deluded self-understanding; against the whole system of false values on which the world for the most part is run. In facing that question mark we come to ourselves and turn to God. All the barriers of pride and self-justification are broken down and we rejoice in him.

In God, forgiveness and reconciliation are one. God's forgiveness is just God taking us to himself, and reconciliation is the way this breaks down our resistance and turns us to him. This is achieved at a price, the cross. It is not *by* a price, for there is no price to be paid either to God or anyone else. But it was *at* a terrible cost. As Austin Farrer put it:

> In the saving action of the incarnation God came all lengths to meet us, and dealt humanly with human creatures . . . He came among them, bringing his kingdom, and he let events take their human course. He set the divine life in human neighbourhood. Men discovered it in struggling with it and were captured by it in crucifying it. What could be simpler? And what more divine?[9]

And in the words of a famous hymn by Isaac Watts:

> When I survey the wond'rous Cross
> On which the Prince of Glory died,
> My richest Gain I count but Loss,
> And pour Contempt on all my Pride.

We might then pray:

> Jesus, crucified and risen,
> dispel the mist of our self-deception and collusion in the
> world's delusions.
> Break down all the barriers of pride and self-justification
> that separate us from you,
> We rejoice that in your eyes we matter so much, are of such
> worth, that you reached out to us even to death on the
> cross.
> Help us to come to our senses and move at one with your
> music now and for ever.

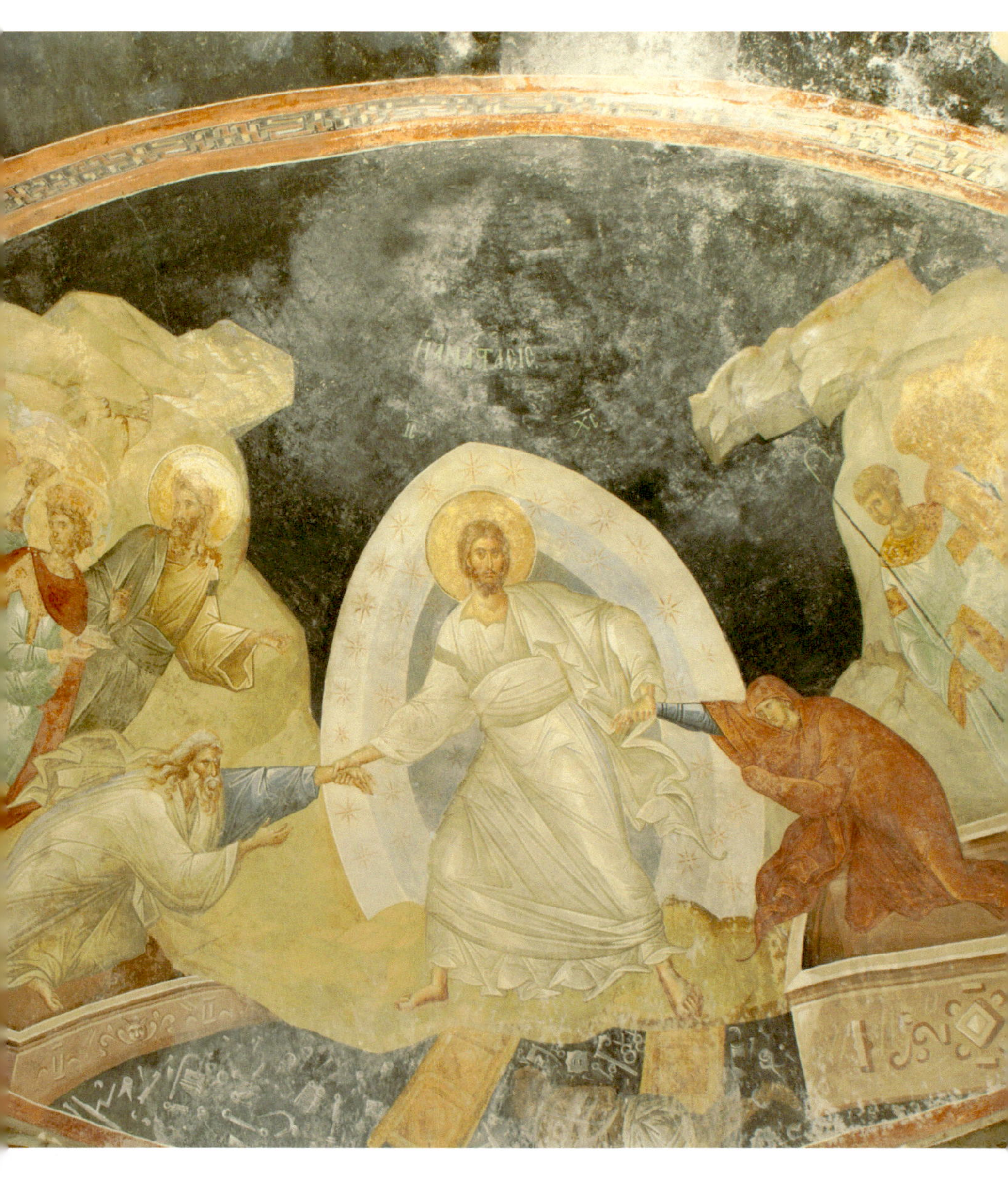

Η ΑΝΑCΤΑCΙC
IC   XC

19

Delivered from darkness

The Anastasis, fourteenth-century fresco

The earliest proclamation of the Christian faith said that Christ 'was raised to life on the third day' (1 Corinthians 15.14). In fact what happened on the third day – that is, Sunday, the first day of the week and the third day after Jesus was crucified – was that the women found his tomb empty. Christ clearly rose from the dead before that.

The early Church was always very reticent about that profound mystery, and it was not represented in art. However, at the Renaissance artists loved to show Christ rising out of a marble tomb. These are often beautiful paintings, but for some people, including me, they create a very misleading impression.

The Orthodox Church was much wiser in depicting the resurrection (*anastasis* in Greek) symbolically, as in this fresco in the Church of the Chora (now the Kariye Mosque), Istanbul. Christ is shown entering the realm of the dead and releasing the departed not only from death but from the power of evil. On Christ's right Adam is being pulled out, while above him John the Baptist points to Christ. Behind him are two kings, David and Solomon, indicating Christ's royal human descent. To the left of Christ are Eve and Abel, the first person to be murdered, whose innocent blood cried out to God. Behind them are prophets of old. Below Christ's feet we can see the broken gates and bars of hell. Christ himself is portrayed in a bright mandorla, with its three rings of light indicating the Trinity. In a version of the Anastasis I have on my mantelpiece, Adam is looking up at Christ who shines in the surrounding darkness. In the version reproduced in this book, I love the way Christ is pulling Adam and Eve up to float free into a kind of dance.[10]

This scene, which has some biblical foundation in 1 Peter 3.18–20, was vividly described in the apocryphal Gospel of Nicodemus. In the West, it is known as the Descent into Hell. It finds expression in the poem *Piers Plowman* by William Langland, the mystical writing of Julian of Norwich and also appears in medieval mystery plays. Bellini and Mantegna painted the descent, but from a very different perspective.

The central message of this powerful piece of symbolism, however, is that Christ has entered the darkest places we know or can imagine. I think of someone in despair, perhaps contemplating suicide; or someone with a terrible burden on their conscience, the knowledge of something that they have done to hurt someone else. Christ is there with us in such darkness with the promise that the power of evil, all sin, and death itself, have been defeated.

Visually and liturgically it is the Christian East that most powerfully conveys a sense of the whole of creation being altered by the Anastasis: of some fundamental shift in the foundation of things; of a descent to utter darkness that, through the resurrection, has united even the most estranged of creatures with God now and for ever. The service of Mattins on Holy Saturday in the Orthodox Church puts it this way:

> To earth hast thou come down, O master, to save Adam,
> and not finding him on earth, thou hast descended
> into hell, seeking him there.
> Uplifted on the cross, thou hast uplifted with thyself all
> living men; and then descending beneath the earth
> thou raisest up all that lie buried there.
> The whole creation was altered by thy Passion; for all
> things suffered with thee, knowing, O Lord, that thou
> holdest all in unity.

Christ not only enters our darkness, he is with us there holding us to God. Psalm 139 says:

> If I go down to hell thou art there also . . .
> If I say, peradventure the darkness shall cover me: then
>   shall my night be turned to day
> Yea, the darkness is no darkness with thee, but the night is
>   as clear as the day.

And we might pray:

> We lift into your presence, O God, all those in despair, those contemplating suicide, those with a heavy burden on their conscience. Be with them in their darkness and lift them into your light.

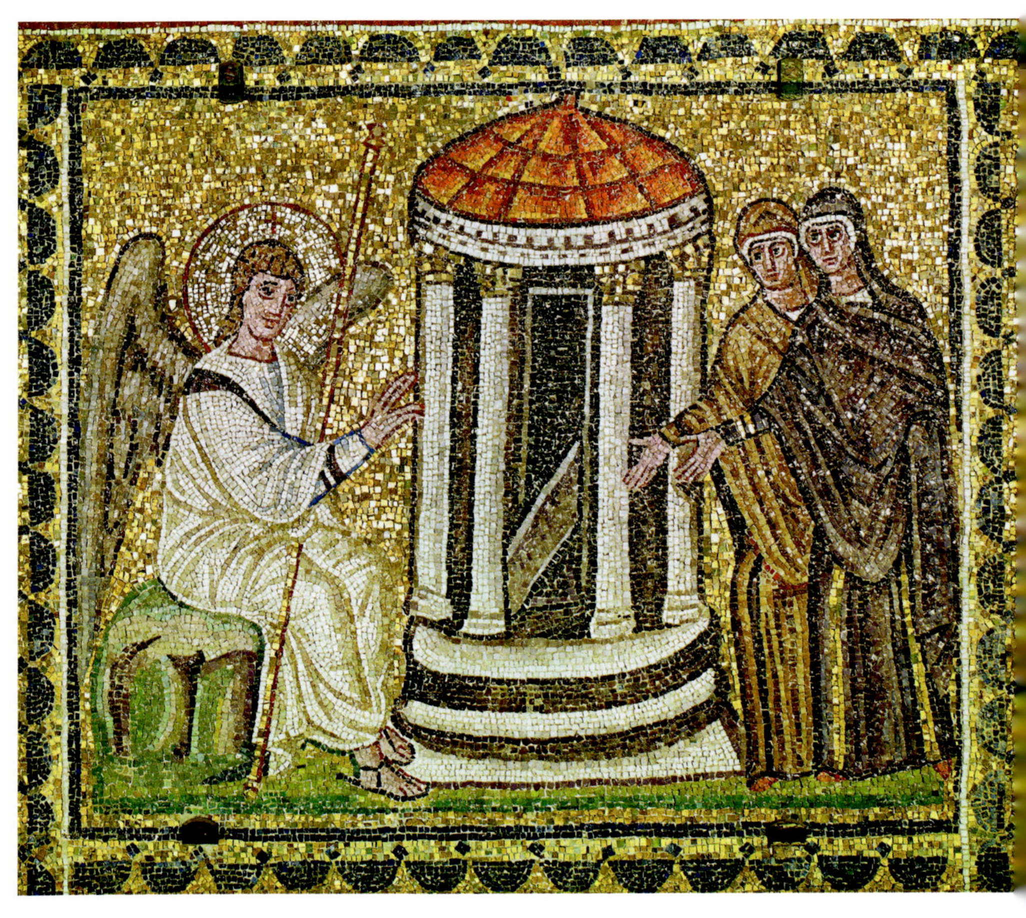

20

'He is not here, he is risen'

The two Marys finding the tomb of Jesus empty, sixth-century mosaic

The tomb of Jesus did not of course look as it is depicted in this mosaic. The tomb shown here is the monument built in the Church of the Holy Sepulchre in Jerusalem over the place where Jesus was believed to have been buried. This is what pilgrims to Jerusalem would have seen in the sixth century. They would have been reminded of the story of how some women went to the tomb on the first Easter morning to anoint the body of Jesus and found the stone rolled away (in this mosaic it is a slab). A young man or angel told them Jesus had been raised from the dead. 'He is not here . . . He is going ahead of you into Galilee: there you will see him' (Mark 16.1–16).

Belief in the resurrection of Christ is based upon two claims: that the tomb was found empty and that his followers experienced his living presence. St Paul wrote:

Now, brothers and sisters, I want to remind you of the gospel I preached to you, which you received and on which you have taken your stand. For what I received I passed on to you as of first importance: that Christ died for our sins according to the Scriptures, that he was buried, that he was raised on the third day according to the Scriptures, and that he appeared to Cephas, and then to the Twelve. After that, he appeared to more than five hundred of the brothers and sisters at the same time, most of whom are still living, though some have fallen asleep. Then he appeared to James, then to all the apostles, and last of all he appeared to me also, as to one abnormally born. (1 Corinthians 15.1–5, NIV)

This was written about the year AD 53. However, it contains the Greek words for receiving and passing on a tradition. In other words Paul is recounting a message that went back to the earliest days of the Church.

The tomb of Jesus was found empty and no body was ever discovered. There are two important considerations here. First, that the enemies of Jesus never produced his body. They could quickly have demolished the Christian message if they had, but this never happened. Second, if some follower of Jesus had secretly taken his body to honour it, a memorial would have been erected, like others in Jerusalem at the time. There never was such a memorial.

These two considerations do not of course prove that Jesus was raised from the dead, but they do show that alternative explanations have little validity. On the other side there is the undeniable fact that a small group of utterly broken men, and some women, who had fled the scene in horror, most of them going back to Galilee where they came from, experienced something that not only turned their lives around but impelled most of them to give their lives to share the good news with others.

According to the historian E. H. Carr, history is a continuous interaction of the present with the past, and furthermore that the facts we select and how we interpret them depend on the presuppositions of the present. This obviously includes both the zeitgeist of our culture and our own assumptions. So, first we have to ask: what is the mindset of those approaching the claim that Jesus was raised from the dead? If we come with a totally closed mind, with the certainty that such a thing could not possibly happen, then of course we can never come to faith.

The philosopher David Hume asserted that, on the balance of probabilities, in the light of other miraculous claims that we know to be false, it was much more likely that the disciples were under an illusion than that what they said was fact. But this brings out the important point that the resurrection of Christ was not a miracle like other miracles. The first Christians claimed it was a new creation. It was comparable only with the origin of the world in the first place, when matter appeared *ex nihilo*, out of nothing, and the end of the world, when the whole of creation would be changed into the stuff of immortality.

This in turn leads us to the presuppositions of those first followers. Why did they interpret what happened in the way they did? They were of course Jews. They believed in a God who acted in history. They believed that God had chosen the Jewish people for a particular purpose. They had believed that this purpose was coming to a climax in the ministry of Jesus, his teaching about the kingdom of God, his healing and his call for people to follow him. All those hopes seemed totally dashed by his being tortured to death on the cross.

Then they suddenly experienced his living presence with them. Their prior beliefs influenced the way they understood this experience and reaffirmed what they had started to believe, namely that God was indeed acting in Jesus to bring in his kingdom. At the same time, it forced them to see that God's purpose was not an easy earthly triumph, but one brought about by suffering through death. They looked again at the Hebrew scriptures and found within them passages that did seem to point to such a startling conclusion.

Those were the presuppositions the disciples brought to bear in interpreting their experience of the living Lord and the claim that the tomb had been found empty. So what about our prior assumptions?

St Paul wrote, 'For you were buried with him in baptism, and in that baptism you were also raised to life with him through your faith in the active power of God, who raised him from the dead' (Colossians 2.12). And again, 'Were you not raised to life with Christ? Then aspire to the realm above' (Colossians 3.1). In other words, the risen Christ was understood to be not just a person to whom believers could pray but a reality in whom they had become incorporated. They too had been raised to new life, Christ lived in them and they in him. The prior assumption that those Christians brought to bear was this mystical participation in Christ's risen life. It was in that light that they heard again, and later read, the first stories of the finding of the empty tomb and the encounter of Peter, Paul and others with the risen Lord.[11]

After the Easter period in the Church's calendar come Ascension Day and Whitsun, and these reveal another important aspect of Christian truth. In the period immediately after the crucifixion his followers had particularly vivid experiences of the presence of the Jesus they had known in his earthly ministry. Ascension and Whitsun indicate the fact that this intense, vivid presence only lasted for a short period. Most Christians hereafter would know Jesus in a new way, not as a localized presence but through the Spirit of God in the deepest part of their hearts. Jesus was raised to a universal contemporaneity. In the immediate aftermath of his death this was sharply focused in a local presence, but then he was released from the bounds of space to be present with everyone, everywhere. The encounter of the risen Christ with the first followers took place in relation to the particular circumstances and challenge of their lives, most dramatically when Peter was given the opportunity to say three times that he loved Jesus, to match his threefold denial. Now he meets us in the circumstances and challenges of our lives, through the illumination of our minds by the Holy Spirit.

This is a prayer of Brother Roger of Taizé:

O Christ tirelessly you seek out those who are looking for you and who think that you are far away: teach us, at every moment, to place our spirit in your hands. While we are looking for you, already you have found us. No matter how poor our prayer is, you listen to us far beyond what we can imagine and believe.

Part 3

IN CHRIST

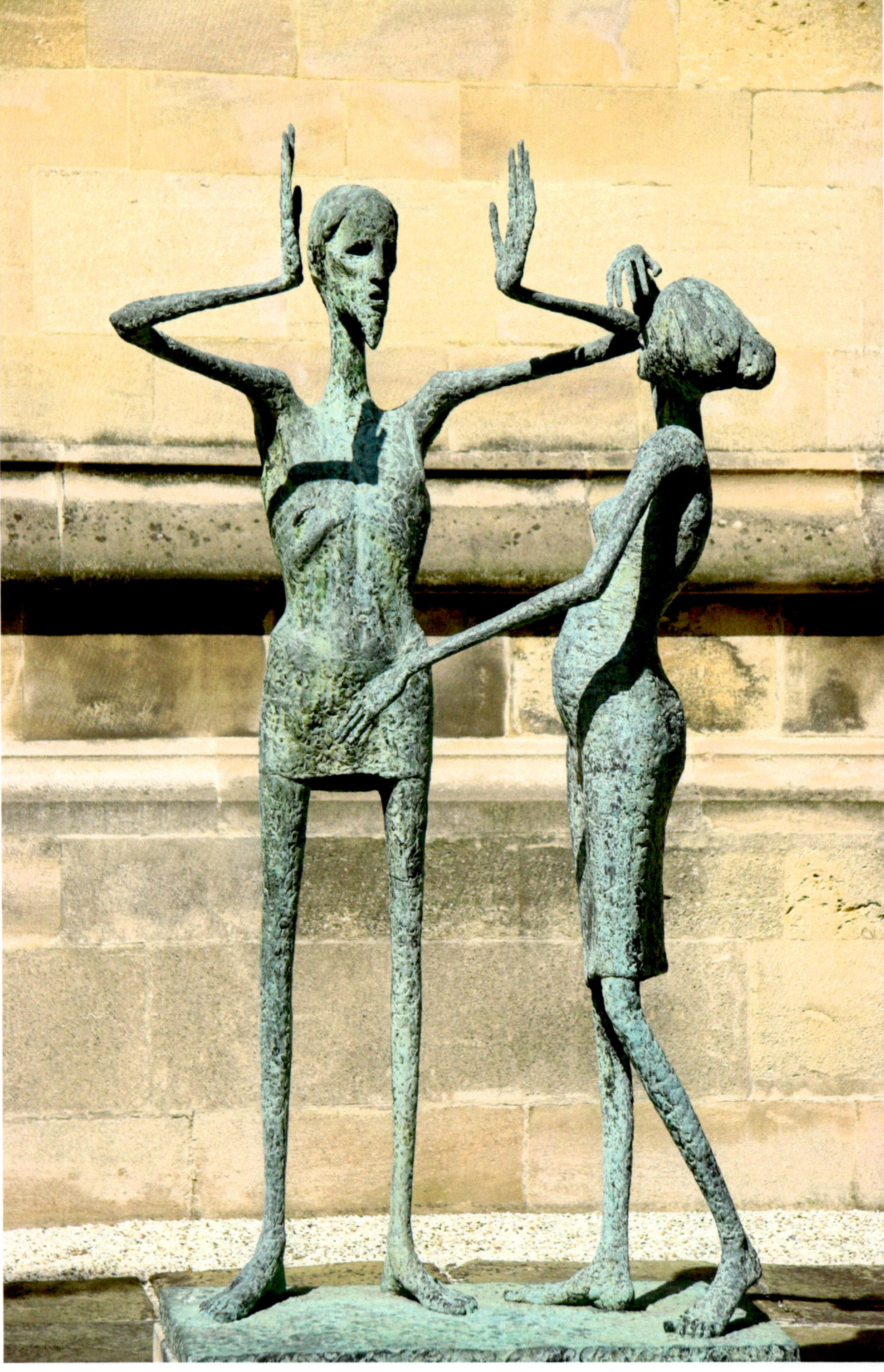

21

'Do not cling to me, I have not yet ascended to the Father'

David Wynne, *Noli me tangere*, 1963

This sculpture captures the moment when Mary Magdalene encounters the risen Christ in the garden outside his tomb. She reaches out to touch him but he says to her, 'Do not touch me, I have not yet ascended to the Father.' Famous paintings of the scene, for example by Fra Angelico and Titian, depict Mary reaching out and Jesus turning away. This work by David Wynne (1926–2014), which stands in a small courtyard in Magdalen College, Oxford – a version can also be seen in Ely Cathedral – captures well the words that follow: 'Go to my brothers and tell them I am ascending to my father and your father, to my God and your God' (John 20.10–18).

The hands of Jesus are pointed heavenwards and Mary is looking at his face. Her arms, instead of reaching forward to touch Jesus, are relaxed, forming part of the upward movement of her body. It as though Christ is actually ascending at that moment and Mary is being drawn into a spiral to dance with him. In the image reproduced here the dark shadow behind Mary contrasts with the bright light behind Jesus and shining on his face, and highlights the sense of divine revelation. She, looking up, is almost shielding her face from the glare.

Scholars have often discussed what Jesus meant by saying 'Do not touch me'. The clue is given by some of his earlier words, when he promises he will be with his followers in a way that will be permanent. They will have a joy that can never be snatched away, a peace the world cannot give. This presence will be manifest after the Ascension and the coming of the Holy Spirit, through whose power Christ will dwell in their hearts. That is why he says 'Do not cling to me', as one modern translation puts it, 'For I have not *yet* ascended to the Father.' The word 'yet' is important, for the time will come when his followers will indeed be able to cling to him. He will be present in a new way, in their hearts.

That is why modern translations, such as the aforementioned 'Do not cling to me' (REV), or 'Do not hold on to me' (NRSV), convey the sense better than the older one, 'Do not touch me'. It is not yet the time of Jesus' permanent presence, so his followers are not to hold on to him now. That is to come shortly when he has ascended to the Father and sent the Holy Spirit. Then he will not be just a local presence in Jerusalem, but present with everyone in every age. He will be present as God is present, everywhere. As William Temple, a former Archbishop of Canterbury, once wrote:

> The ascension of Christ is his liberation from all restrictions of time and space. It does not represent his removal from the earth, but his constant presence everywhere on earth. During his earthly ministry he could only be in one place at a time. . . . But now he is united with God, he is present wherever God is present; and that is everywhere. Because he is in heaven, he is everywhere on earth; because he is ascended, he is here now. In the person of the Holy Spirit he dwells in his church, and issues forth from the deepest depths of the souls of his disciples.

The other remarkable feature of the risen Christ's words to Mary is the way he calls his disciples 'Brothers', or as we would gloss it, 'Brothers and sisters'. Although he is the eternal Son of God – indeed *because* he is the eternal Son of God – he takes us into that intimate relationship of kinship with himself. This is further accentuated by the fact that he refers to 'My father and your father, my God and your God'. He is taking them into the same relationship with God that he himself eternally enjoys: that of a beloved daughter or son.

The followers of Jesus in his earthly ministry knew someone they could recognize by the sight of his figure and the sound of his voice. They could touch and feel him and know it was Jesus and not someone else. They were convinced that the one they met after his death was the same Jesus, the same but changed. But the Jesus who is not only risen, but risen, ascended and glorified, is not a localized past figure of history like that. He is present in the turmoil and challenges of our own lives in our own time. He speaks to us not in Aramaic, but in our own tongue; not through sound waves, but through the thoughts of our mind as we respond to our daily experiences.

How do we know that this is indeed Jesus, and not just our own fantasies? There is only one way, and that is by allowing our thoughts and deeds to be more and more shaped by the words of Scripture within the loving community of a Christian congregation. Of course there is no escaping the fact that all our thoughts about God will to some extent reflect our own limitations and weaknesses, our hopes and fears. But a Christian will be aware of this, and will seek more and more to be shaped and suffused by God's disclosure of himself in Jesus. In him the heart of God is made accessible in human terms, and his life, now taken into eternity, has a contemporary relevance for every human being in every situation. It is in the interaction of that life and our own concerns, through the inspiration of the Holy Spirit within us, that we discover God's purpose and ways for our own lives.

We rejoice O Christ that you call us your brothers and sisters, and that in union with you we can live as sons and daughters of eternal love. Through the power of your spirit help us to dwell in that love, and live it out towards those we meet today.

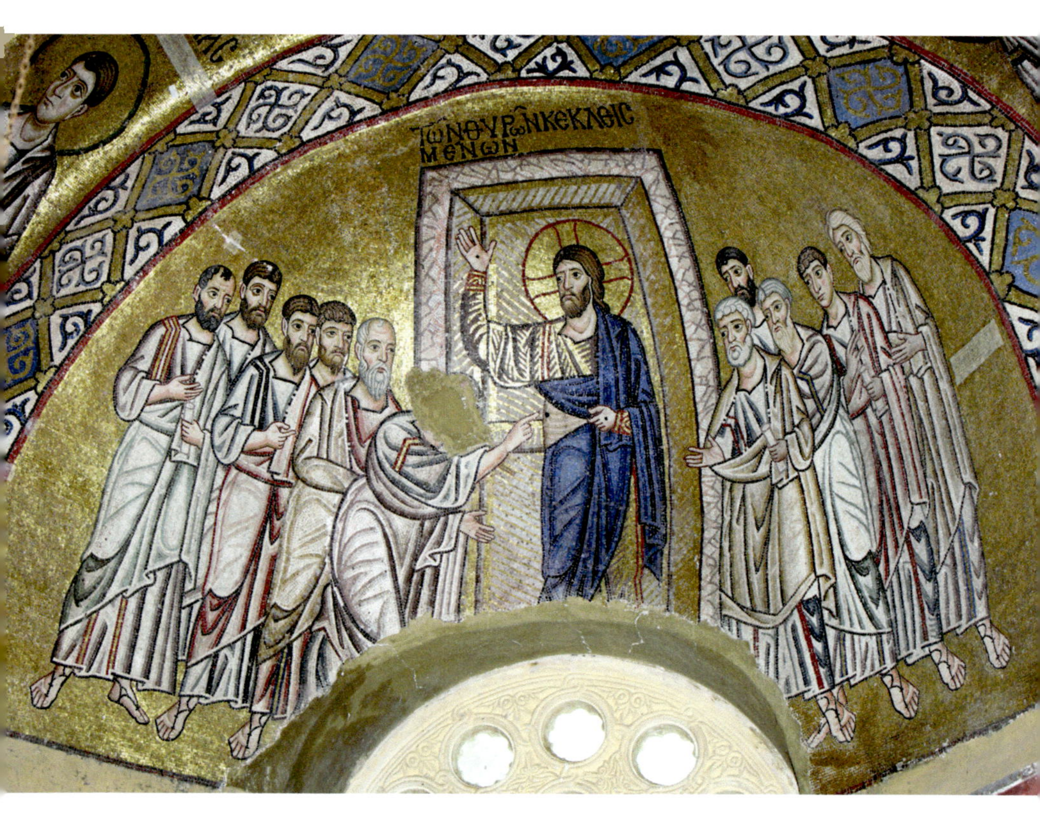
ΤΩΝ ΘΥΡΩΝ ΚΕΚΛΕΙϹ
ΜΕΝΩΝ

22
Questioning

Mosaic at Hosios Loukas, Greece, c. 1120

One of my favourite places is the walled monastery of Hosios Loukas, above the Bay of Corinth, about two hours' drive from Athens. It contains a number of superb mosaics and frescoes, of which this is one. After Jesus had been raised from the dead he appeared to a group of disciples who, out of fear, had locked themselves in a room. One of the disciples, Thomas, however, was not with them, and when he heard about their claim that Jesus had risen from the dead, he was sceptical. Later Jesus appeared to Thomas too and invited him to feel the wounds in his hands and side. Thomas needed no more convincing, and he exclaimed 'My Lord and my God' (John 20.24–29).

In this mosaic, Jesus holds his hands open and shows his side so that the wounds can be clearly seen. Thomas stares (his face sadly damaged) at the wound in Jesus' side, though he does not actually put his hand in as he is depicted doing in a dramatic painting by Caravaggio. There are 11 apostles, Judas having deserted them, with their vivid faces and classical flowing robes. Most dramatically, Jesus appears against the background of a closed door that is also the shape of a sarcophagus, as though to stress that he has risen from the dead.

Thomas was surely right to question the claim of the other disciples. They had experienced something; at that stage he had not. Questioning is not only a good thing to do, but is essential. All advances in science, and in scholarship more generally, have come from people's willingness to challenge accepted views. All changes for the better in the way we live have come about from people's discontent with the way things are. The willingness to question is fundamental to religious understanding as well. How can we come to believe something, or believe something with deeper conviction, unless we are willing to probe and question what is claimed to be true?

There is a fine hymn that contains the line 'Faith believes nor questions how.' I always change it to 'and questions how'. Anselm (1033–1109), a very great Archbishop of Canterbury, wrote a book titled *Fides quarens intellectum* – faith seeking understanding. It is in the nature of faith to seek deeper understanding. That means probing and questioning. People sometimes ask a believer, 'Do you have doubts?' But doubt is not the right word here, or a very helpful one. What the believer should be fully conscious of are the arguments against what she or he believes.

Those arguments and challenges to the faith will be held in tension with believers' religious conviction. Indeed, as T. S. Eliot argued, following the French philosopher Pascal, the more mature one's faith, the more intense will be one's awareness of the challenges to that faith. This is not to say that people do not lose their faith. They do, and it can be a devastating experience. For such individuals, life is thought at one moment to be the creation of a wise and loving power, and then at the next it all seems a meaningless horror. Serious atheists will see and feel something of both sides of this mystery, the mystery of life itself. They will feel the strength of the horror because they can imagine the pull of its opposite, faith in a loving God. That is why the serious atheist and the serious Christian sometimes feel close.

Many people, of course, do not like to think of these matters at all. The implications are too great and threatening, so they immerse themselves in their busy lives. Some take up the superficial atheism that is such a feature of our own times, based as it is on a false view of science. In debates with Richard Dawkins, who is a brilliant writer on science itself, I have often had to say. 'Richard, there are so many serious arguments against religious belief. Why do you have to keep dragging science into it?' Scientists believe and disbelieve like any other human being. They bring their total life experience to bear on the matter. The really challenging argument against the Christian faith, as well as Judaism and Islam, is of course the severity and extent of suffering. This challenge never goes away, even if the arguments I have explored in earlier reflections enable one to live with it.

This discussion of questioning illuminates the fact that religious faith, though rooted in conviction, primarily entails commitment to a way of life. It involves regular prayer and meditation, attendance – at least for Christians – at the Eucharist, and a disciplined lifestyle in relation to the use of money and sexual expression. Above all it is a practical commitment to the well-being of others. At the intellectual level, questioning can and should continue. This will be part of a way of life rooted in a growing conviction built up by experience. As the remarkable French thinker Simone Weil wrote:

> It seemed to me certain, and I still think so today, that one can never wrestle enough with God if one does so out of pure regard for the truth. Christ likes us to prefer truth to him because, before being Christ, he is truth. If one turns aside from him to go toward the truth, one will not go far before falling into his arms.[12]

We could pray for the Lord's guidance:

> Jesus, you are the way, the truth and the life.
> So lead us in your truth
> that we may walk in your way
> And walking that way know the life which nothing can
> take away.

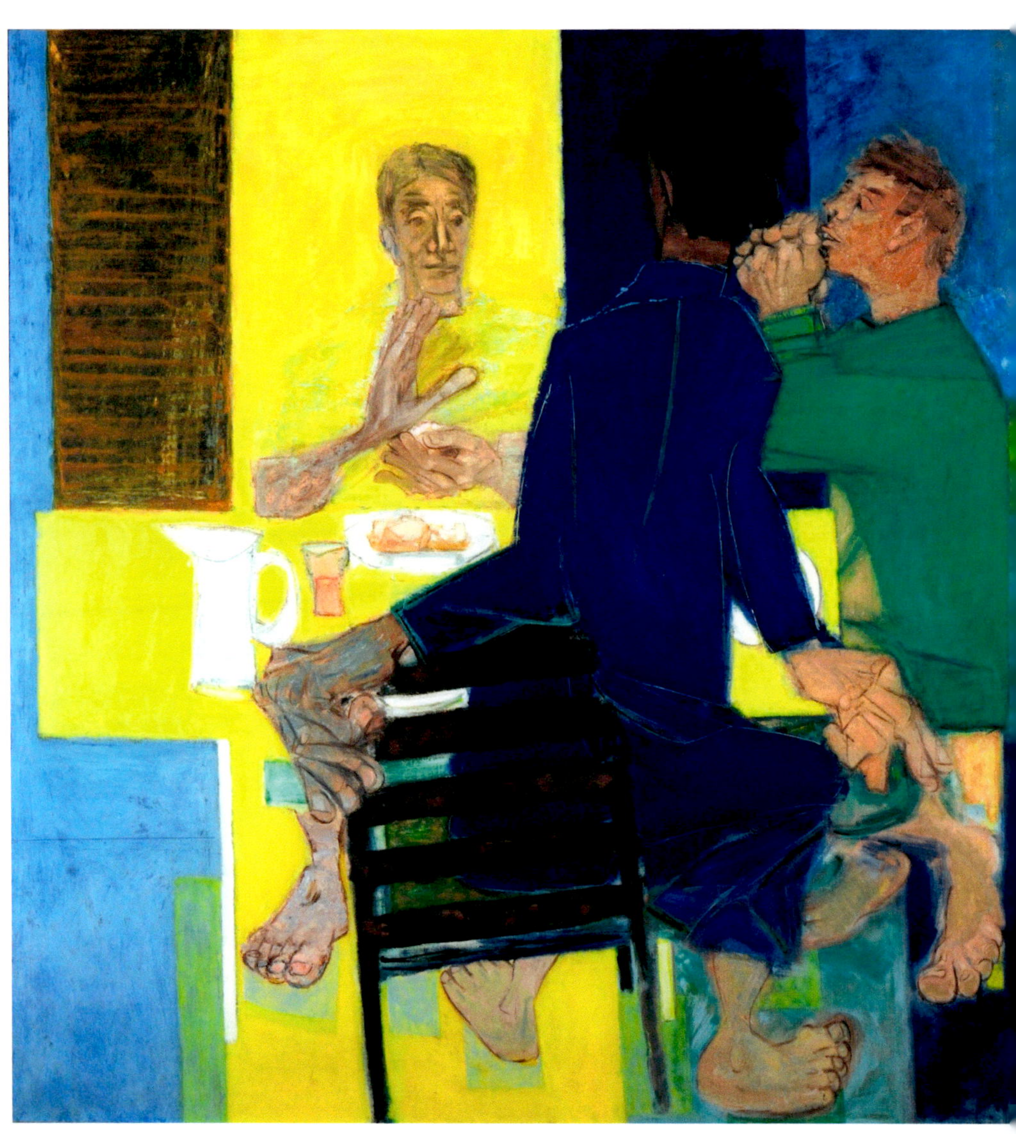

23

The supper at Emmaus

Ceri Richards, *The Supper at Emmaus*, 1958

The story of the appearance of the risen Christ to two of the disciples falls into two parts. First there is the actual journey to Emmaus. The two disciples are on the road when a stranger joins them. They talk about recent traumatic events and the stranger directs them to the Hebrew scriptures to show that the Messiah must suffer before entering into his glory. Second comes the actual supper, particularly the moment when the two disciples recognize the stranger to be Christ (Luke 24.13–35).

At the time of the Counter-Reformation, when the Eucharist became subject to renewed attention, this scene became particularly popular among Christian artists, one famous example being a painting by Caravaggio. This modern rendering by Ceri Richards (1903–71) is no less striking. Commissioned by the Junior Common Room of St Edmund Hall, Oxford, it was placed in the chapel to celebrate the acceptance of the Hall as a recognized college of the university. It now stands above the altar.

Luke records that 'Their eyes were opened and they recognised him; and he vanished out of their sight'. In Ceri Richards's portrayal, Christ is seated against a great yellow cross of light that at once outlines him and allows him to melt into it. The light is crucial. Here it is not shining on Christ but behind him, forming the background out of which he emerges: the light of eternity in which he is momentarily figured as a human face and form.

The two disciples react to the revelation of Christ in different ways. One rises awkwardly, pushing the chair aside. The other, seated at the side of the table, is disturbed but uncomprehending; his clasped hands are pressed to his mouth in the gesture of a man slow in thought, trying to gain time to readjust his mind. It is a powerful image in which the sudden apprehension of one disciple and the delayed recognition of the other are juxtaposed.

The most unusual feature of the painting, however, are the large hands and feet of both the disciples and Christ himself, made unusually prominent by the figures' narrowed wrists and ankles. The moment of recognition of the risen Christ is also the moment of realization that Christ's work continues through human hands and feet. The hand that raised to bless and teach is a hand that will henceforth work through those large, ungainly yet beautiful extremities of flesh and blood. It has been suggested that it is the imaginative, centrifugal movement of the hands and feet that serves to interrelate the figures, giving them a buoyancy that is itself half suggestive of resurrection. Christ in his risen body gives them the blessed bread, his body broken for humanity, that they might become his risen body in the world.

This story has always been highly significant for Christians as a record not only of the experience of two disciples on the way to Emmaus, but of Christians' experience in every age. For Christ is known and formed in us in two main ways: through reading and reflecting on Scripture and at the eucharistic gathering when we receive Christ in the sacrament. In the Emmaus story, one of the disciples says after the moment of recognition: 'Were not our hearts on fire as he talked to us on the road and explained the scriptures to us?' Countless Christians have felt that same sense of excitement when Scripture comes alive for them as a source of inspiration, strength and guidance for their life. In a related way, countless Christians feel that, as they receive Holy Communion, their holy union with God in Christ is sustained and renewed.

When Oscar Wilde was in jail he used to read a few verses of the New Testament in Greek every morning. It was a time when he thought very seriously not only about his own life but about Christ. In his deeply moving essay *De Profundis*, which came out of that experience, he wrote: 'Once in his life every man walks with Christ to Emmaus.'

Open our eyes O Christ that we may discern you
in the people we meet,
the meals we share,
the words we read
and the solitude of our own hearts.

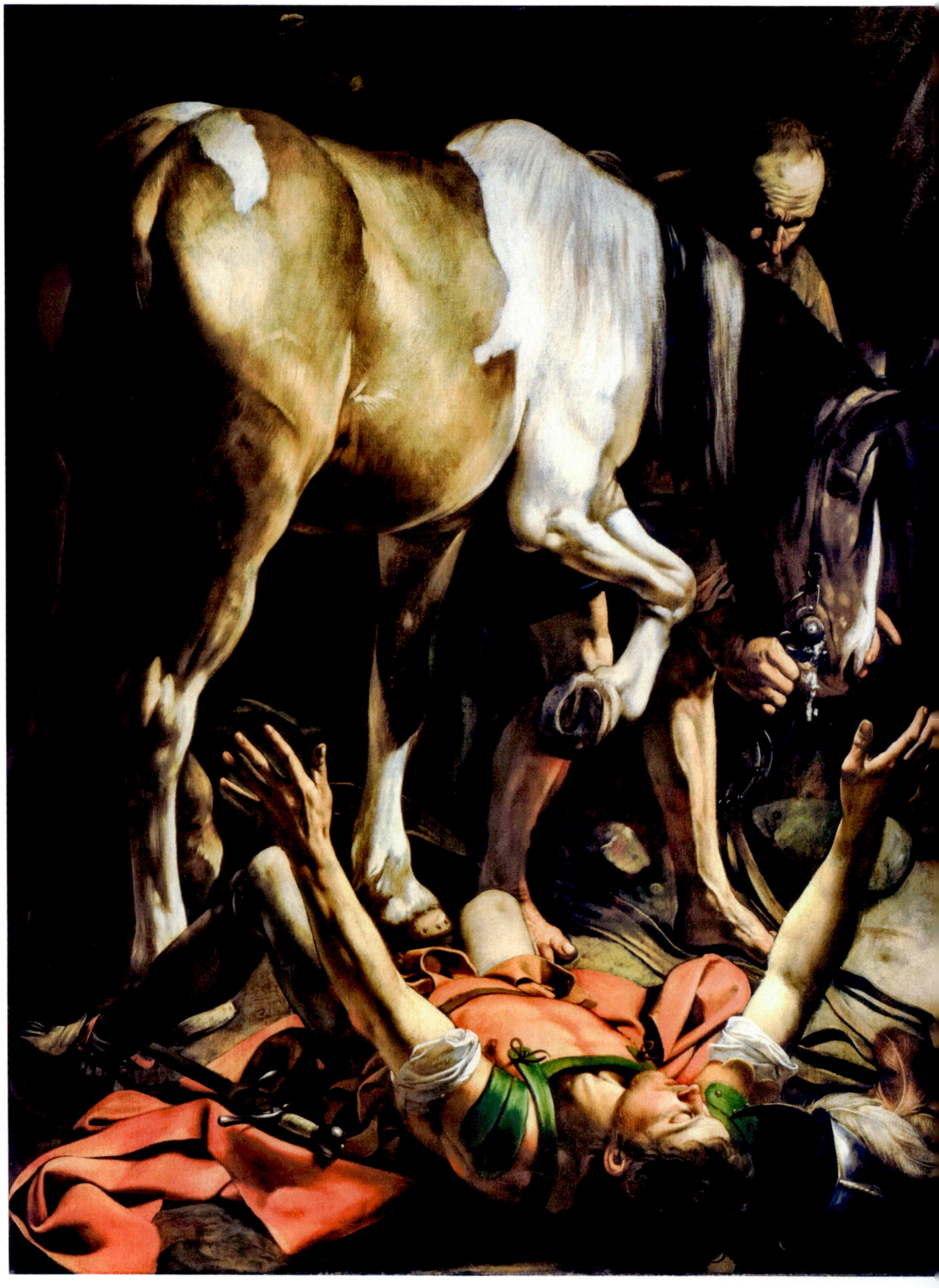

24

Life turned upside down

Caravaggio, *Conversion on the Way to Damascus,* 1600–02

In his earlier life, Saul was not someone we would have felt comfortable with. He was not the kind of person you would invite in for a meal. It was not just that he was deeply religious, he was a fanatic. He was, I'm afraid, willing to kill people whose religion he disagreed with. He was what today we would call a jihadist. When the first of his fellow Jews started to become Christians, he was so outraged that he set off for Damascus to capture some of those who had gone there. On the journey something extraordinary happened to him. It turned his life upside down (Acts 9.1–9; see also Galatians 1.13–17).

Caravaggio (1571–1610), the painter of the scene reproduced here, was another man who led a tempestuous and traumatic life. He was even accused of murder. In all his paintings on Christian themes, not least in this one, there is a great sense of drama. Saul has been thrown from his horse and lies on the ground blinded, his arms flung upwards as he hears a voice speaking to him. Even the horse, with its hoof lifted high over Saul's face, seems dangerous.

What Saul heard were the words, 'Saul, Saul, why are you persecuting me?' It was in fact Christian believers that he was persecuting, so it is noteworthy how closely the risen Christ identified himself with his followers. From that moment Paul, as he became, devoted his life to teaching people about how God, in Christ, had come to save us from our own self-destruction. Like so many of the early Christians, it would cost him his life.

Because of his influence on the early Church, and on Christian thinking in subsequent generations, especially at the time of the Reformation, Paul is arguably one of the half dozen most influential figures in human history. He wrote most of the letters in the New Testament and is the central figure in the first history of the early Church, the Acts of the Apostles, which tells the story of his mission all over the Mediterranean world.

In Paul's writings there is still a touch of the old Saul, an occasional defensiveness or boastfulness or fierceness. But he has fundamentally changed. The way he cares about the small congregations he has founded is often deeply moving, and there are many sublime passages, not least his well-known hymn to love in the thirteenth chapter of his first letter to Christians at Corinth.

Plenty of people in history have had their lives turned around in a dramatic way like St Paul. Some undergo a conversion as teenagers when they first start thinking whether life has any meaning or purpose. Others have such an experience in mid-life, when they may have become dissatisfied with an active outer life and start looking for deeper inward things. Some people undergo a conversion after being addicted to drugs or alcohol, or after a breakdown in relationships. Many, however, have been brought up as Christians and God has been part of their life from an early age. For them there has been a gradual growing in the faith.

Whether a person has had a conversion experience or has gradually grown into a personal faith, however, nobody changes totally overnight. The slave trader John Newton, for example, was converted to Christ, but it took him some time to realize that enslaving others was a terrible sin. The fact is that we need to turn away from ourselves and put ourselves in the hands of Christ, not just once but again and again. For we find time and again that we are in fact being driven by our own ego and not by love of God and other people. At such times we discover once more that God takes us as we are. Faith is about our acceptance of God's acceptance of us even as we discover some less acceptable side of ourselves. There may be times when, in the words of a confession in *Common Worship*, we want to say:

> Forgive what we have been,
> help us to amend what we are,
> and direct what we shall be;
> that we may do justly,
> love mercy,
> and walk humbly with you, our God.

I love these words from Psalm 80:

> Turn us again O God,
> Lift up the light of your face upon us
> That we may turn and be whole.

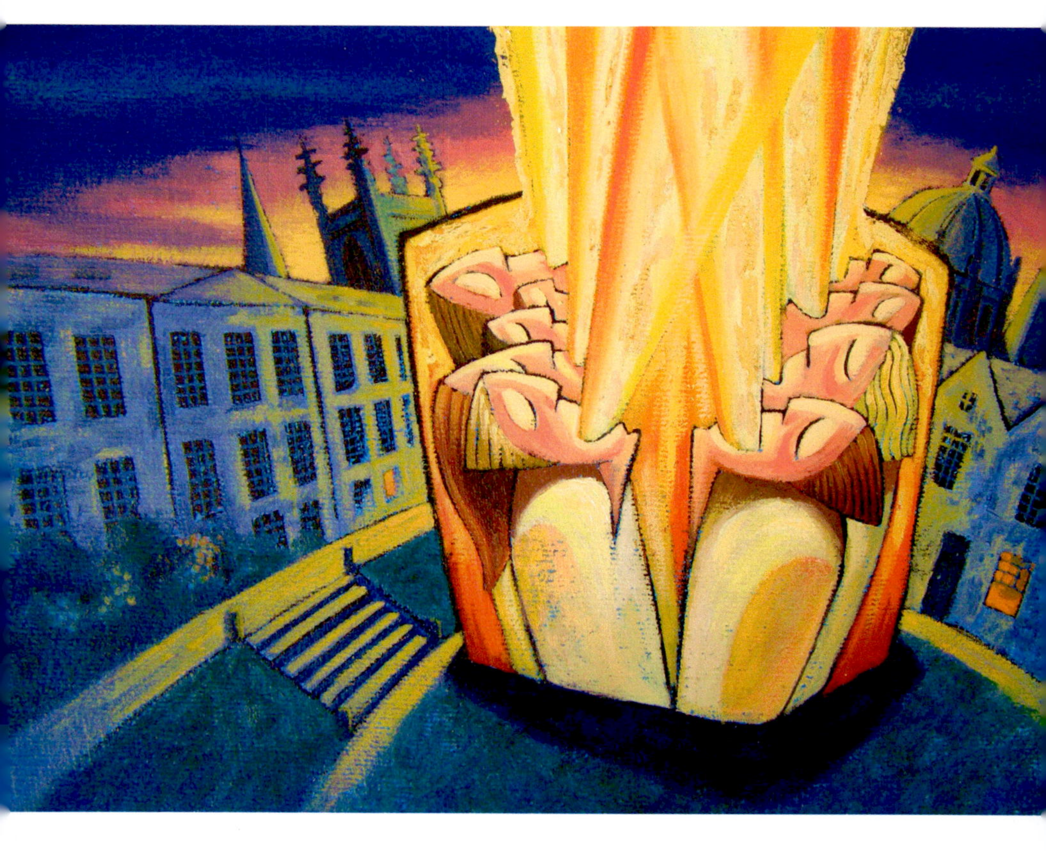

25

The Spirit descends to live within us

Nicholas Mynheer, *Worcester College Chapel Choir*, 2003

When I first saw this image, it brought to mind a famous scene from the second chapter of the Acts of the Apostles. The passage describes how, seven weeks after Jesus was raised from the dead, his followers had the most extraordinary experience. They were all together in one place when they heard a strong, driving wind making a noise that seemed to fill the whole house: 'And there appeared to them flames like tongues of fire distributed among them and coming to rest on each one. They were all filled with the Holy Spirit.' This Spirit enabled them to preach the gospel in a way that could be understood by the crowds present whatever their native language.

In this painting Nicholas Mynheer (b. 1958) has for me captured the moment when flames of fire pouring down from heaven enter the mouths of the apostles. He has chosen their mouths rather than their heads, for it is from their mouths that the words of the gospel will come. The apostles' faces are turned upwards, eyes closed, as in a rapture. Mynheer depicts the apostles all huddled together in a small space; for although we are often on our own, Christian life is essentially life with others and for others: 'Where two or three are gathered together in my name, there am I in in the midst of them' (Matthew 18.20, KJV). And where Christ is, there is his Holy Spirit.

In Christian tradition fire is a symbol of the love of God that enflames our hearts with love. It is an image wonderfully explored in one of the most accessible of T. S. Eliot's verses in 'Little Gidding', the last of his *Four Quartets*.[13] The Spirit descends to live within us and lift our hearts to God. So, in Mynheer's painting, the streams of fire are also the songs and praise of the chapel choir going heavenwards. When I came across the image for the first time, not knowing its title, it seemed a wonderfully arresting depiction of the first Pentecost, as described above. The title indicates that it is in fact a choir singing. But the two belong together. It is only through the Spirit that our prayer and praises arise.

When God said 'Let there be . . .' he gave the whole universe a life of its own, as discussed in the first reflection in this book. There is a sense in which he put human life outside himself. In an old Jewish myth, God withdraws himself to leave a place where he is not, so that life independent of God can exist. Except, of course, that no life can be independent of God. Moment by moment he holds us in being. Furthermore, it is the good purpose of God not only to give us life but to fill us with his own life.

God is poised ready to fill us with that life and love. He is not only the ground of our being but also a spring ready to well up inside us. But the way through is blocked. Spread on the ground of our being is a sludge of old leaf litter and mud, formed from all those attitudes that close us in on ourselves: our self-absorption, self-justification, self-pity and self-seeking at the expense of others. Christ came to clear all that muck away. As we turn to Christ and look at him looking at us, the spring of God's Spirit wells up inside us. His friendship allows that spring to flow within. United with Christ, the spirit within reaches out to the Father.

The workings of the mind are very mysterious. Thoughts and feelings arise unseen and unsought. They are suddenly *there*. As we examine those thoughts before God and think through them as honestly and seriously as we can, suffusing them in prayer, we can,

Christians believe, often find God's guidance for our lives. This does not mean bypassing the use of our minds. It means using the rational side of us, before God and with God. Christians believe, too, that in this way they can find fresh resources of strength to go on when life is difficult. They believe that prayer itself is God's Spirit working in us. As St Paul wrote:

> We do not even know how to pray as we ought to pray, but through our inarticulate groanings the Spirit himself is pleading for us, and God who searches our inmost being knows what the Spirit means because he pleads for God's own people as God himself wills.
> (Romans 8.26–27)

And elsewhere:

But as it is written:

'Eye has not seen, nor ear heard,
Nor have entered into the heart of man
The things which God has prepared for those who love Him.'

But God has revealed them to us through His Spirit. For the Spirit searches all things, yes, the deep things of God. For what man knows the things of a man except the spirit of the man which is in him? Even so no one knows the things of God except the Spirit of God. Now we have received, not the spirit of the world, but the Spirit who is from God, that we might know the things that have been freely given to us by God.
(1 Corinthians 2.9–12 NKJV)

This Holy Spirit helps us to make good decisions, gives us strength to implement them and keeps us close to Christ.

O Holy Spirit, giver of life and light,
Impart to us thoughts higher than our own thoughts,
Prayers better than our own prayers,
Powers beyond our own powers,
That may spend and be spent in the ways of love and goodness,
After the perfect image of Jesus Christ our Lord.

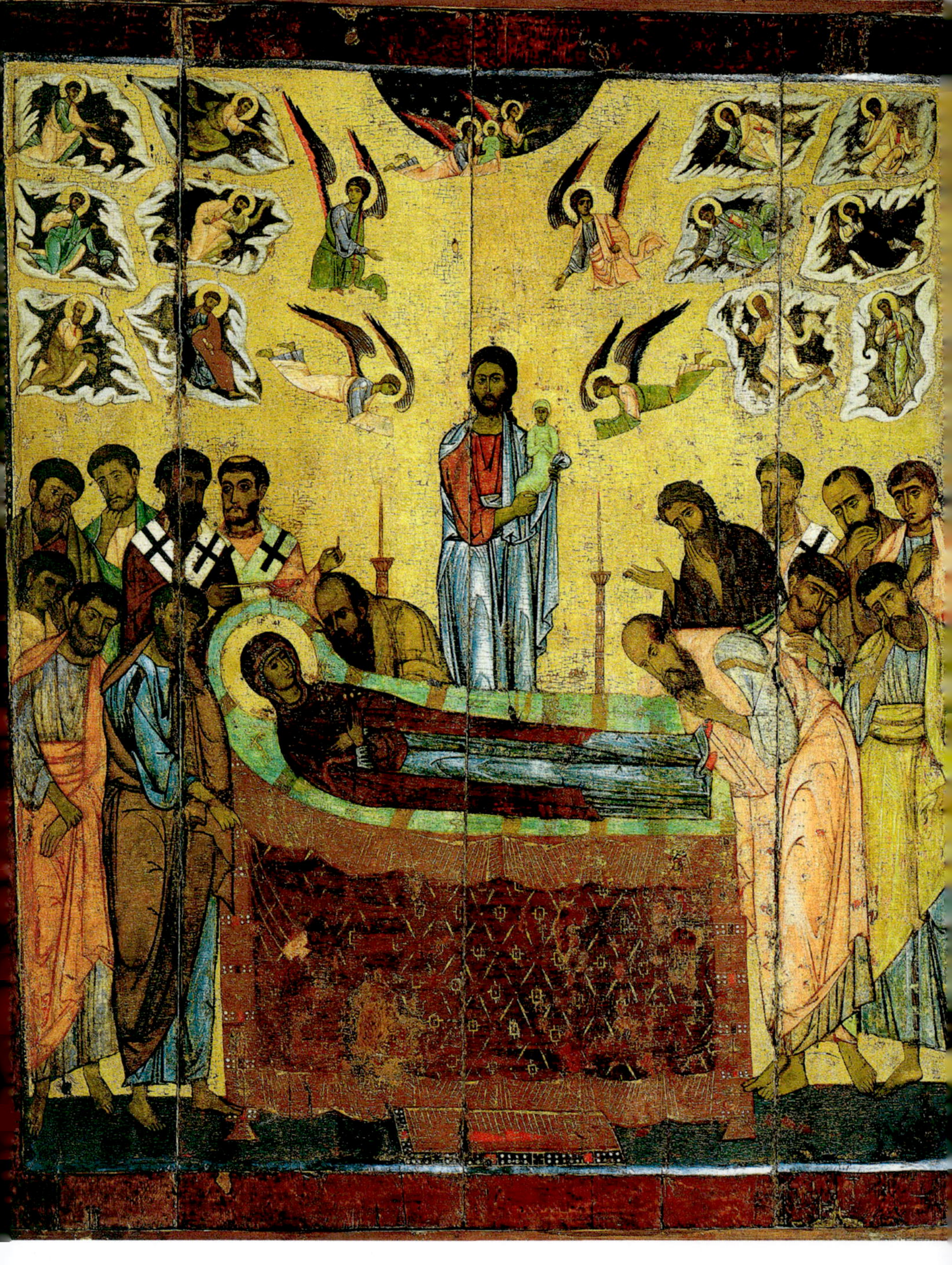

26

The dormition of the Blessed Virgin Mary

Twelfth-century icon

The death of the Virgin Mary, who is given the title Mother of God in the Roman Catholic Church and Theotokos, or God-bearer, in Orthodox churches, is not recorded in the New Testament. From the fifth century, however, various accounts were written of the end of her earthly life. According to one tradition the apostles were miraculously transported from different places to be with her.

In this icon, for example, it is possible to recognize Paul, with his large bald pate, at the foot of Mary as she lies dying. What I particularly love is the figure of Christ holding the infant Mary, symbolizing her soul, which she is carrying into heaven. At the top of the icon, that same figure is being taken into the circle of heaven. In the Roman Catholic Church and the Orthodox churches, the day of Mary's falling asleep, or dormition (*koimesis* in Greek), is a major feast celebrated on 15 August. (For those following the Julian calendar it is on 28 August.)[14] Roman Catholics normally call this day the Feast of the Assumption.

This image of Christ carrying the soul of Mary into heaven raises many questions for the modern mind. What is a soul? Do we have one? We know that we are psychosomatic unities: that body, mind and soul are bound up together. So when the body dies it would seem that the whole of us goes to dust. There is no box inside a box inside a box. No wispy, invisible something that lives on. This should not in fact trouble us too much, for the Christian hope is primarily focused on the belief that the essential person we are, our true self, is known to God, and as known to God, is lodged in his heart, even when we die. So that essential self can be recreated and clothed in immortality, in a form that fits a new mode of existence. It is this idea of resurrection that is primarily emphasized in the Bible. The idea of an immortal soul emerges only later in Scripture and was combined, rather uneasily, with the idea of resurrection in Christian thought.

So what does talk about the soul signify? Two things. First, it safeguards the fact that as whole persons, psychosomatic unities, we have an inescapable spiritual orientation and destiny. Our lives originate with a divine initiative and find their fulfilment in the divine purpose. Second, as in the course of our life we develop and grow, we retain a sense of ourselves. We have memories of ourselves as a child and at other stages in our life. We are aware that some of the characteristics we had earlier in life are still with us. Of course we change physically all the time, most obviously as we begin to show signs of old age. But at reunions of old friends after many years, it is usually possible after a moment or two to recognize that overweight, balding person in front of you as the fellow student you played sport with 50 years ago. Often it is the voice that is familiar, sometimes a particular look or smile. There is a noticeable continuity, a distinctive self that we are aware of in ourselves and which can be recognized by others. The swaddled infant Mary in this icon symbolizes her essential self, the self that is known fully only to God, and which Christ is taking to himself.

I also love the way in this icon the apostles are gathered around Mary, while the top half is filled with angels and saints. Death in the modern world can sometimes be a solitary affair. In ancient accounts of the death of holy men and women, however, their friends are shown crowding round the bed, while just the other side of the threshold, as it were, the blessed departed hover ready to welcome the dying one home. There is a mixture of sadness and joy; grieving among the friends and rejoicing in heaven.

There is a prayer that I always like to use at funeral services. Based upon an ancient commendation, it was expanded by Cardinal Newman in his great verse work *The Dream of Gerontius* and set to music by Edward Elgar. The prayer, a version of which is now included in *Common Worship*, was used at Princess Diana's funeral, and it conveys a wonderful sense of ingathering. The red carpet of paradise is laid out with friendly hands either side ready to welcome the departed home.

Go forth upon thy journey from this world, O Christian soul,
In the peace of him in whom thou hast believed,
In the name of God the Father, who created thee,
In the name of Jesus Christ, who suffered for thee,
In the name of the Holy Spirit, who strengthened thee.
May angels and archangels, and all the armies of the
     heavenly host, come to meet thee,
May all the saints of God welcome thee,
May thy portion this day be in gladness and peace and thy
     dwelling in paradise.
Go forth upon thy journey, O Christian soul.

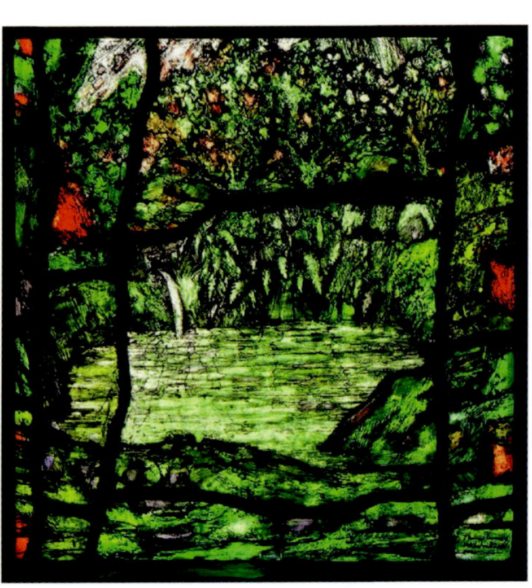

27

Christian mindfulness

Tom Denny, Window in memory of Thomas Traherne, 2006–07

This stained-glass window by Tom Denny (b. 1956) in Hereford Cathedral is part of a memorial to the poet and mystic Thomas Traherne (1636–74). Its vibrancy and intensity, expressed in colour and line, together with its luminosity, capture well something of Traherne's vision of the world. In an example of the intense perception of the world that continues for 100 meditations, and is also reflected in his poetry, Traherne writes that when he was a child,

> The corn was orient and immortal wheat, which never should be reaped, nor was ever sown. I thought it had stood from everlasting to everlasting. The dust and stones of the street were as precious as gold: the gates were at first the end of the world. The green trees when I saw them first through one of the gates transported and ravished me, their sweetness and unusual beauty made my heart to leap, and almost mad with ecstasy, they were such strange and wonderful things . . .

Most of us do not experience the world in this way. We stumble through the days half awake, preoccupied with our own concerns. Occasionally we realize we are missing out on what life has to offer and try to do something about it. Some people, mistakenly, try drugs to lift them into an ecstatic state or mood. Much more sensible is the modern movement of mindfulness. This has as its first objective the stilling of the body and mind, perhaps through appropriate posture and rhythmic breathing – what used to be called 'centring'. After that it means living out the day with greater conscious awareness of sights and sounds, of oneself and others. This is a discipline that is now widely valued in education and healthcare and many people are beginning to find it helpful.

The immediate catalyst for modern mindfulness is Buddhism, but such an approach to life is also deeply grounded in traditional Christian spirituality. From a Christian perspective, three points might be made. First, the object is not to induce a particular state of mind or experience, but to be more aware and appreciative of what is around us and in ourselves. Seeking a particular experience for its own sake, whether ecstasy, peace of heart or well-being, is the wrong way to go about it. Such states of mind come as the fruit of something else, of being drawn out of ourselves to notice and wonder and imagine what is outside our own mind. That's why there is often such a close connection between this kind of perception and poetry. Great poets like Gerard Manley Hopkins, as in his poem beginning 'Glory to God for dappled things', get us to see what we had not really seen before, as do some artists. The object is not to savour our own emotions but to appreciate what is there and exult in its presence for what it is, in its unique 'thisness'.

A second point for Christians is that it is not just the world around us that we seek to be more aware of, but the reality in which that world is grounded and which lies at its heart. Brother Lawrence (Nicholas Herman of Lorraine, 1614–91) was a lay brother at a Paris monastery. He was converted at the age of 18 when he saw a tree in winter stripped of its leaves and thought of how it would be renewed and spring to life again; it spoke to him of the power of God. He spent the whole of his life helping in the monastery kitchen, but his words were collected in a short book, *The Practice of the Presence of God*, which explained what his life meant for him. He wrote:

> We can do little things for God; I turn the cake that is frying on the pan for love of Him, and that done, if there is nothing else to call me, I prostrate myself in worship before Him, who has given me grace to work; afterwards I rise happier than a king. It is enough for me to pick up but a straw from the ground for the love of God.

Many Christians have tried to follow Brother Lawrence's simple advice simply to practise the presence of God. Another person from whom people have learnt much is Father Jean Pierre de Caussade (1675–1751). The heart of his teaching is equally simple and similarly challenging:[15] we are to practise what he calls 'The sacrament of the present moment'. As we saw in an earlier reflection, a sacrament is defined by the Church of England as something outward and visible with an inward and spiritual meaning. Sacraments do not belong only to the Church; in a fundamental sense the whole world is sacramental. Similarly, every moment is a sacrament. If we live fully in the moment, we live aware not merely of the outward nature of things, but of their wider meaning and purpose.

This leads to the third point a Christian might make. At the heart of the universe is not only a beauty that draws us out of ourselves to appreciate both what is around us and the beauty from which it springs forth but also a moral imperative that calls us to grow in love to others and God in response to his unlimited love for us in Christ. In a Christian vision, aesthetics, spirituality and ethics belong together in the source of all beauty, truth and goodness. In response to this, Christians try to live out the words of St Paul, to 'pray without ceasing' (1 Thessalonians 5.17, NKJV).

The stained-glass window reproduced here captures beautifully something of Traherne's intensity of vision, the heightened awareness that can come about as a by-product of Christian mindfulness. It vividly reflects some words of Traherne himself:

Thus did I by the water's brink
Another World beneath me think;
And while the lofty spacious Skie
Reversed there abus'd mine Eys,
I fancy'd other feet
Came mine to touch and meet;
As by som puddle I did play
Another World within it lay.

Our prayer could be:

Open our eyes and ears O God that we may be more aware
of the world about us

Open the eyes of our hearts that we may be more aware of
you in all things.

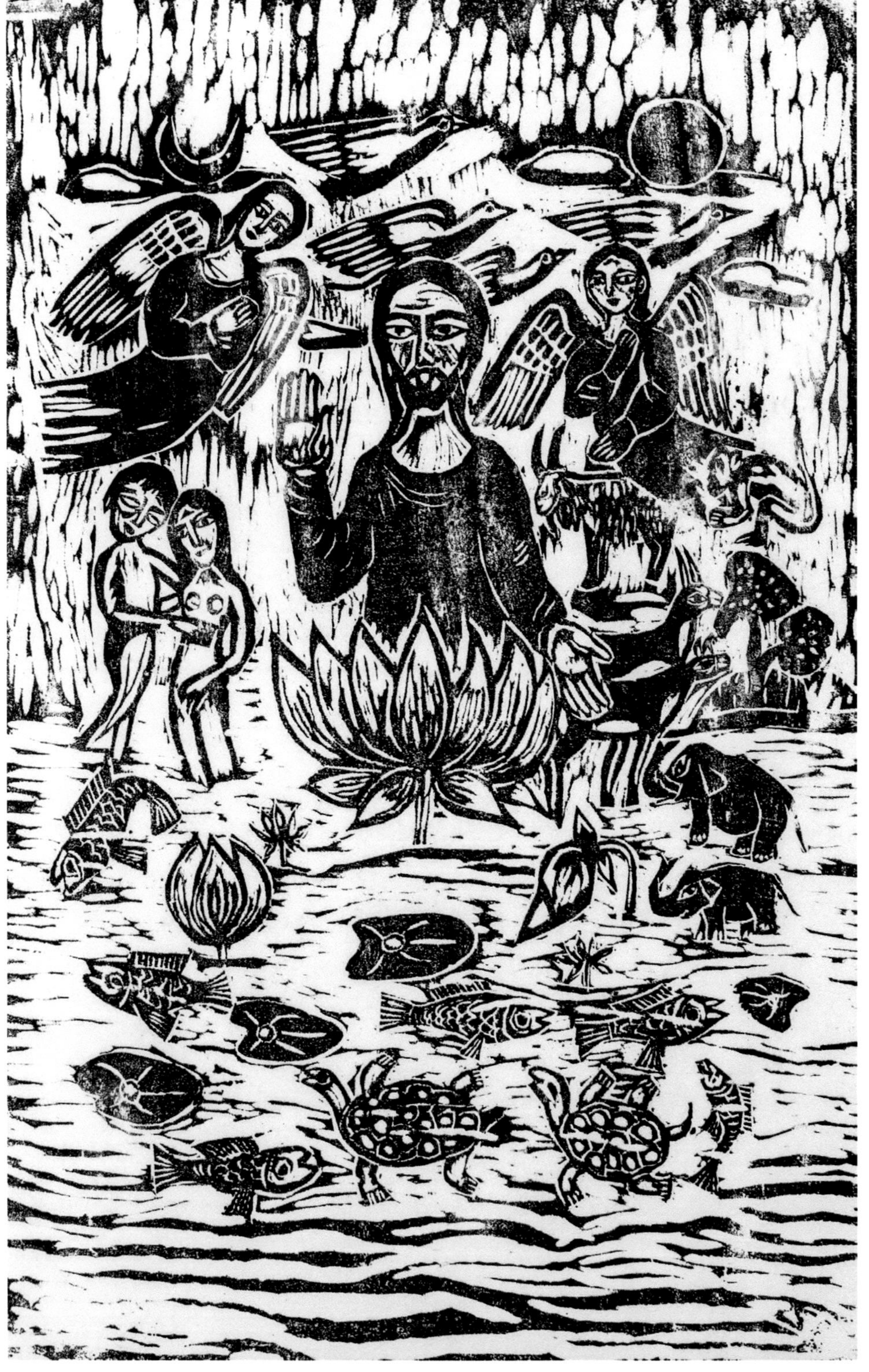

28

'Christ within us, our true self'
Solomon Raj, Etching, c. 1995

In much of the religion and culture of Asia, the lotus plant is a symbol of our true, deepest, eternal self. In this lithograph by the Indian painter and academic P. Solomon Raj (b. 1921), Christ is shown arising from the lotus, one hand raised in blessing of the world, and the other, with palms open, receptive to it. There are resonances with Buddhism in his gestures. Around the figure all creation is depicted in harmony, the fish in the river and the birds in the air; the animals and plants on the land. Adam and Eve are shown in a gentle protective embrace. This earthly realm is at one with the angelic, heavenly realm symbolized by the angels.

For 50 years or more people in Western societies have been told 'Be yourself.' But what is this self we are told to be? We have been encouraged to be 'authentic'. But does that simply mean expressing every impulse within us? Being rude to others just because that is how we feel, because to refrain from doing so would be false to what we are feeling? The ancient religions of India have a profounder understanding of what is meant by our true or real self, and the lotus is a wonderful symbol of this.

St Paul wrote, 'This is the secret hidden from the ages and now revealed: Christ in you, the hope of Glory' (Colossians 1.27). As mentioned in an earlier meditation, there is a well-known prayer in the Book of Common Prayer that ends with the words 'That we may dwell in him and he in us.' For Christians, our true self is nothing less than Christ within us; a Christ who is formed daily as we seek to live in him and follow him in the way of love.

We have, however, to acknowledge that most of us have something of a split personality. There is the ego: self-seeking, drawing attention to itself, assertive. Then there is the deeper self which comes through in our better moments. I knew a clergyman once in whom that split was very marked. Amazingly self-centred for much of the time, he liked nothing better than to be at the centre of a group of friends listening to him talk – and he talked very well. Then, in the pulpit or celebrating the Eucharist, all that was put aside and another self seemed to come through in a way which drew people through him into a spiritual reality.

When Dietrich Bonhoeffer was in prison for his part in the resistance to Hitler, he wrote a poem called 'Who am I?' In it he contrasted how others saw him – calm, confident, friendly – with how he felt inside himself: frightened, lonely, full of longing. The poem ends:

Who am I? This or the Other?
Am I one person today and tomorrow another?
Am I both at once? A hypocrite before others,
And before myself a contemptible woebegone weakling?
Or is something within me still like a beaten army
Fleeing in disorder from victory already achieved?

Who am I? They mock me, these lonely questions of mine.
Whoever I am, Thou knowest, O God, I am thine![16]

I love those last lines. We don't really know who we are, but God does, and we belong to him. We can put our trust in him and he will make us truly who we are.

No one has put the idea of our true self being Christ within us better than Gerard Manley Hopkins. In his poem 'As kingfishers catch fire', he describes everything in nature 'doing its own thing', as people sometimes say:

Each mortal thing does one thing and the same:
Deals out that being indoors each one dwells;
Selves – goes itself; *myself* it speaks and spells,
Crying *What I do is me: for that I came.*

He goes on to consider human beings, writing:

I say more: the just man justices;
Keeps grace: that keeps all his goings graces;
Acts in God's eye what in God's eye he is –
Chríst – for Christ plays in ten thousand places,
Lovely in limbs, and lovely in eyes not his
To the Father through the features of men's faces.

It is true for humans as well as for the rest of creation that 'What I do is me: for that I came.' But that me becomes more me as it becomes more transparent to Christ. For Christ is our soul's soul, our true centre. Being oneself means resting in and living from that centre.

On you alone, O Christ, my soul in stillness waits.
In you alone, O Christ, my soul in stillness rests.
So live in me that I may live in you.

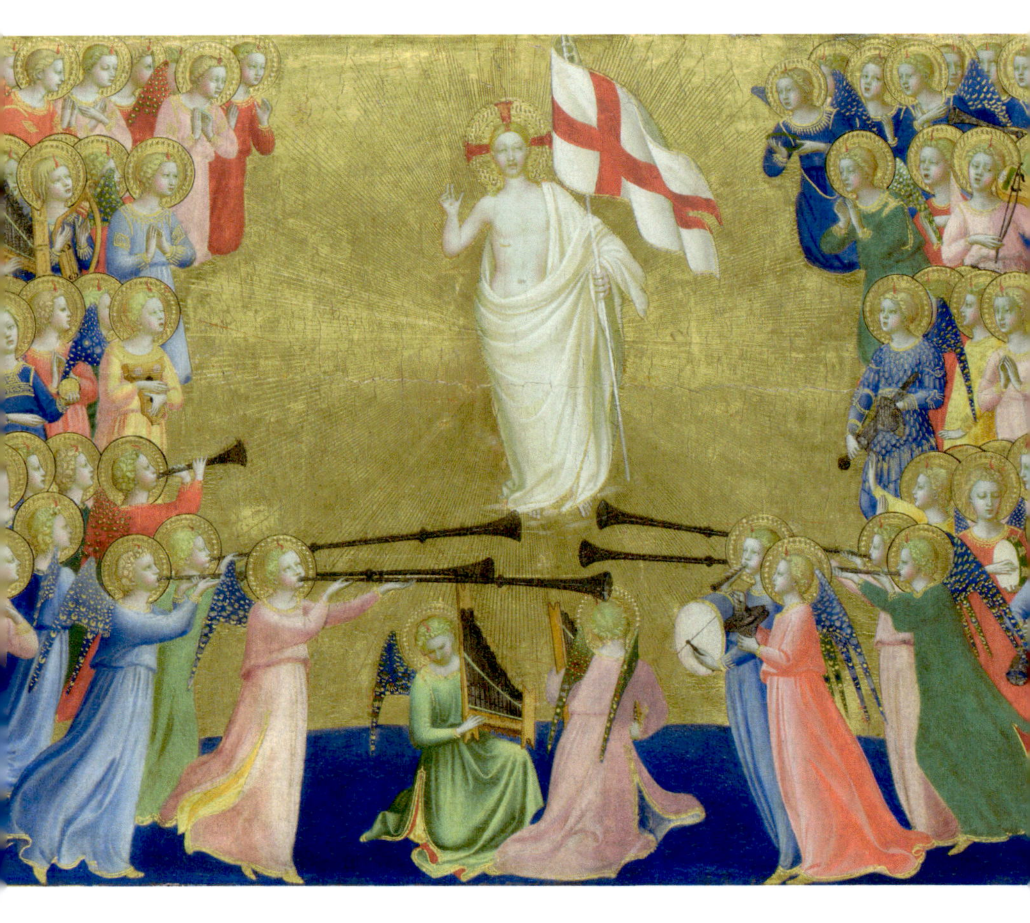

29

The Communion of Saints

Fra Angelico, *Christ Glorified in the Court of Heaven*, c. 1423–24

This painting by Fra Angelico (1395–1455) is greatly and rightly admired as a work of art. It conveys a wonderful sense of joy, ecstasy, music, movement and dance, all focused on and drawn out by the figure of Christ in the middle. The imagery, however, is strange to most people today. But we can begin to glimpse its meaning for Christians if we think about the concept of evolution. Is life heading anywhere? Is there some great consummation ahead? Some climax beyond space and time?

As mentioned in an earlier reflection, the universe as we know it came into being about 13.8 billion years ago. For many billions of years there was nothing more than exploding matter. Then, about 4.5 billion years ago, in a process that scientists do not yet fully understand, life emerged. As forms of life evolved, they became ever more complex, until about 400,000 years ago *Homo sapiens* arrived on the scene, able to think and choose and manipulate nature in a way we recognize as being in continuity with our own characteristics.

By then, therefore, there had been three big steps: matter, life and mind. Christians believe that this was not the end of the evolutionary process. The next stage, however, was not the result of evolution in nature, but of the human mind being so open to the divine, and so at one with the divine purpose, that mind became God-filled mind. As discussed in earlier reflections in this book, the Christian claim is that Jesus Christ reflected the mind and heart of God. So the sequence now runs: matter, life, mind, God-filled mind.

But this is not the end of it either, for it is the divine purpose to unite with Christ all such human minds as are willing. The consummation of this process lies beyond space and time in what we call the Communion of Saints – a communion of all those bonded and bound together in the love of Christ. People now like to speculate that we could, through artificial intelligence and genetic replacement, live for ever on earth. But the Christian faith holds out a bigger vision: of a life changed and transformed into the kind of everlasting communion of mutual reciprocity that, in our better moments, we would love it to be.

The book of Revelation contains several visionary moments in which the author tries to describe the ecstasy of people taken out of themselves in appreciation, awe and love (Revelation 7.9–17; 21.1–8). Strictly speaking, the Communion of Saints in heaven is way beyond anything we can imagine now. The important points are, however, first, that this is a form of life that includes others. Some people have thought of religion in terms of the alone being present with the alone. But human life is essentially social, and that is as true of heaven as it is on earth.

Second, heaven is a fulfilment of our human longing to be taken out of ourselves in joyous ecstasy. For many people the nearest they come to this is in music, when they feel lost in the music and part of it; some know such joy in the first experience of falling in love. It is not surprising that traditional images of heaven, as in Fra Angelico's painting, depict it as containing musical instruments and choirs. John Donne's prayer expresses the idea well:

Bring us, O Lord God, at our last awakening into the house and gate of heaven, to enter into that gate and dwell in that house, where there shall be no darkness nor dazzling, but one equal light; no noise nor silence, but one equal music . . .

Another characteristic of heaven as traditionally portrayed is of everyone being drawn into a beautiful dance. It is not just that we shall be taken out of ourselves in the music, but that our whole being will move at one with it. This idea of the mystical dance appears both in Sufi literature and the apocryphal *Gospel of Thomas*, as well as in the well-known modern hymn, 'Lord of the Dance'. In Fra Angelico's painting everyone also moves as in a dance.

We should not think of heaven as limited to the canonical saints, to practising Christians, or even just to those we know to be good. As Austin Farrer put it, 'The Sacraments are God's covenanted mercies. Of his uncovenanted mercies there is no end.' In other words, believers who have been baptized and share in the eucharistic fellowship of the Church are promised God's grace. But we can set no limit to that grace. There is a fine phrase in the bidding prayer of the annual Service of Nine Lessons and Carols from King's College, Cambridge: 'All those who rejoice with us but in a greater light on another shore.' That having been said, the Bible is quite clear that Christ presents us with a challenge and a choice – to respond to him now and always in trust, love and obedience.

In the New Testament, ordinary Christians in their congregation are described as 'The saints'. But because Christ has joined heaven and earth in a way that can never be separated, the living and the departed are bound up together in one communion and fellowship. This means that, as we are supported by the prayers of those who love us on earth, so we are supported by the love and prayers of those who are Christ's in heaven. That is why the majority of Christians feel no embarrassment about looking to the saints for help. It in no way detracts from the supremacy of Christ, for his grace works in and through those who are members of his body, whether on earth or in heaven.

In a novel by Susan Hill, a newly bereaved widow is seen going into a church for her husband's funeral. What she became aware of, she realized:

was not the presence of the village people sitting or kneeling behind her, but of others, the church was full of all those who had ever prayed in it, the air was crammed and vibrating with their goodness and the freedom and power of their resurrection, and she felt herself to be part of some great living and growing tapestry, every thread of which joined with and crossed and belonged to every other, though each one was also entirely and distinctly itself. She heard again the strange music in her head and her ears, and yet somewhere far outside of them.[17]

This is an Orthodox prayer, very slightly changed, that I like to say in the mornings. It lifts me into the prayers of heaven as well as joining me to the prayers of my friends on earth:

Christ, the true light,
enlighten all who come into the world.
Lift up your face upon us that in it
we may behold the unapproachable light.
Guide our footsteps in your ways
through the prayers of your most pure mother and all the
    saints.

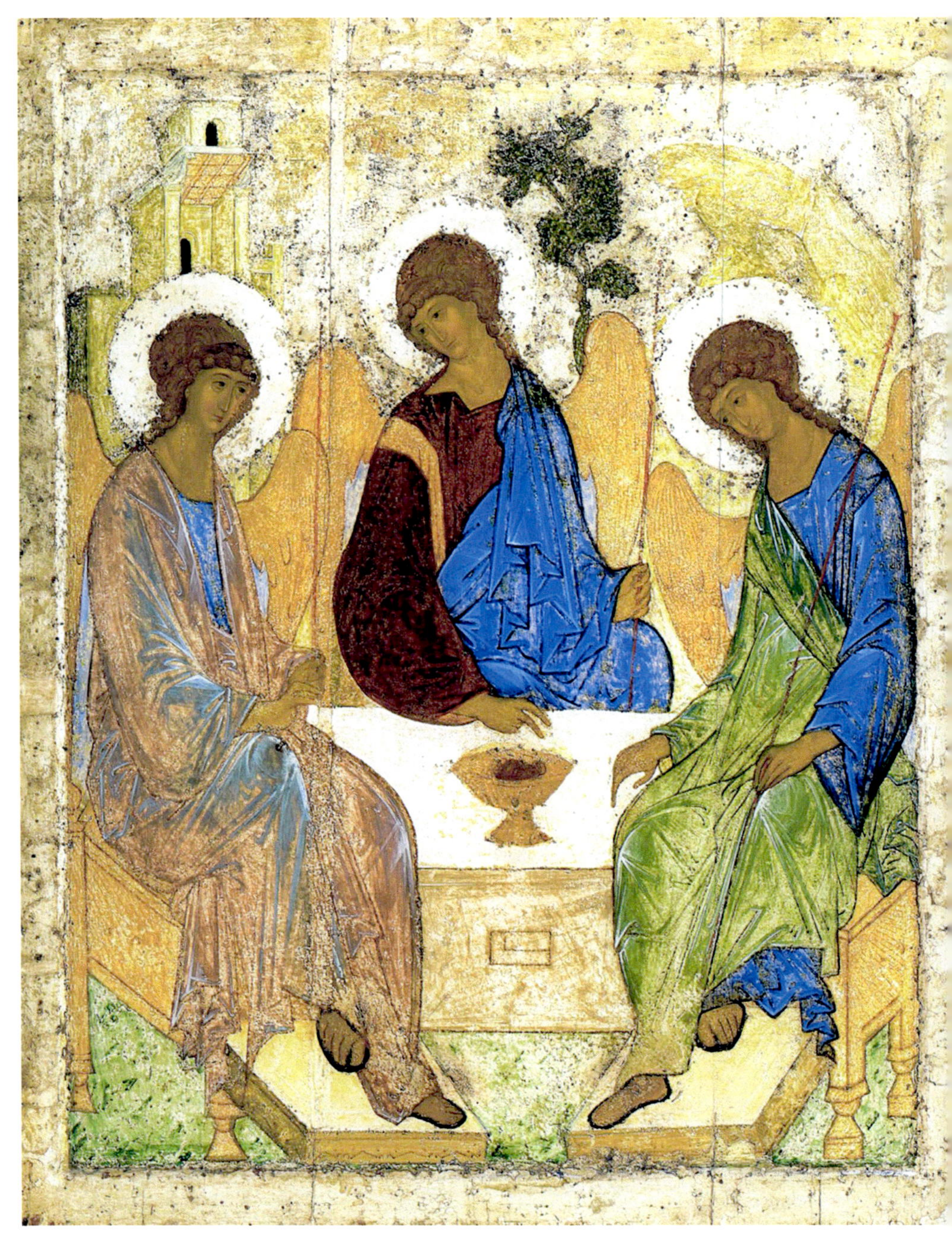

30

The hospitality of God

Andrei Rublev, *The Trinity*, c. 1425–7

I love this icon. First of all for its classical lines, as seen in the elegant, flowing robes of the angels and their serene faces. Here we have a direct link with the classical art of Athens in the fifth century BC. Inherited by the Greek-speaking Byzantine culture based in Constantinople and passed on to Russia, this art found another flowering in the fifteenth century, especially in the work of Andrei Rublev (1360/70–1427/30).

The icon is based on a story in the Hebrew scriptures in which three strangers visit Abraham and Sarah. The couple offer the visitors something to eat and drink, and they turn out to be angels (Genesis 18.1–8). From an early stage Christians saw in this story a pointer to God as Holy Trinity. The earliest depictions of the incident, for example in the wonderful mosaics in San Vitale in Ravenna, show the whole story. However, in Rublev's icon there is no sign of Abraham or Sarah, and the whole focus is on the three angels.

The second reason why I, and so many others, love this icon is because of the sense of harmony, spiritual unity and peace of the angels. They seem to exist in a timeless circle of everflowing love. The angel on the right bends in towards the angel in the centre, who in turn bends towards the one on the left. This angel looks across to the first one, and the flow continues round again. These figures are, as mentioned above, in the tradition of classical sculpture, but softened and made tender by the Christian faith from which they sprang, the faith of Rublev himself and the Christian culture of which he was a part. Here is not just a classical elegance but a spiritual beauty, what the psalmist calls the beauty of holiness, the beauty of divine love ever circling between the Father, the Son and the Holy Spirit.

The third reason this icon means so much is because the viewer seems to be drawn in to sit at the table with the angels. The onlooker sees a gap ahead, as it were an empty space, that she is invited to occupy. This brings to mind not only the Eucharist in which Christians partake, and the heavenly banquet about which Jesus spoke, but also the very life of God. As human beings we are invited to share in the divine life of love, to be filled with it, to let it flow through us to others.

During the Cold War I visited the Soviet Union on a number of occasions, and one time I purchased, for a few roubles, a copy of this famous icon. That copy now hangs in the room where we eat, a reminder that every meal is a sacrament, an invitation to share in the life of God as we share food and talk together. This icon is sometimes called the hospitality of Abraham, but in the hands of Rublev it becomes the hospitality of God. It is God himself who invites us to share in his life.

A much-loved poem of George Herbert takes the form of a dialogue between God and the human soul. Divine love invites the writer to sit at table, but he feels unworthy. The poem, called 'Love', ends:

And know you not, says Love, who bore the blame?
My dear, then I will serve.
You must sit down, says Love, and taste my meat:
So I did sit and eat.

So we could offer the prayer:

God the Father, holding me in being,
God the Son, enfolding me with your love,
God the Holy Spirit, filling me with your wisdom,
One God ever to be worshipped and adored.
So draw me into the circle of your love
that others too may know themselves to be invited in.

Notes

1 Rowan Williams, 'Icons and the Practice of Prayer', in *The Christian Tradition for Today* (London: Bloomsbury, 2017), p. 122. The whole chapter is well worth reading.

2 Sicily in the twelfth and thirteenth centuries was a golden period with a rich mix of Arab, Norman and Byzantine cultures. These mosaics, which cover the whole cathedral, would have been made by craftsmen trained in Constantinople but they show some Western influence.

3 A phrase used by the writer of the fourteenth-century mystical work *The Cloud of Unknowing*, which, he said, we could only pierce by darts of longing love.

4 For further reflection on the relationship between Judaism and Christianity, see Richard Harries, *After the Evil: Christianity and Judaism in the shadow of the holocaust* (Oxford: OUP, 2003).

5 My own attempt to wrestle with this question is Richard Harries, *The Beauty and the Horror: Searching for God in a suffering world* (London: SPCK, 2016).

6 I have written more about Roger Wagner and some of the other artists in this book in *The Image of Christ in Modern Art* (Farnham: Ashgate, 2013).

7 Austin Farrer, *Saving Belief* (London: Hodder & Stoughton, 1964), pp. 74–5.

8 This icon is based on a work by the great master of icon painting Theophanes the Greek (*c.* 1340–*c.* 1410). Theophanes was the teacher and mentor of Andrei Rublev (*c.* 1370–*c.* 1430), who is regarded as the greatest icon painter of Russia's golden age.

9 Farrer, *Saving Belief,* p. 99.

10 For another image, and a discussion of the development of the

Anastasis iconography, see Richard Harries, *The Passion in Art* (Farnham: Ashgate, 2004), pp. 37, 81.

11 Those who would like to see an expanded version of this argument will find it in Richard Harries, *Christ Is Risen* (London: Mowbray, 1988). It is out of print but copies are often available on Amazon.

12 Simone Weil, *Waiting on God* (London: Fontana, 1959), p. 36.

13 T. S. Eliot, *Four Quartets* (London: Faber, 2001), IV, p. 41.

14 The Julian calendar was instituted by Julius Caesar in 70 BC. In 1582, Pope Gregory XIII replaced it in the West with the Gregorian calendar, which is used in most of the world today.

15 A basic introduction to Christian prayer can be found in Richard Harries, *Turning to Prayer* (London: Mowbray, 1978).

16 Dietrich Bonhoeffer, *Letters and Papers from Prison* (London: Fontana, 1959), p. 173.

17 Susan Hill, *In the Springtime of the Year* (London: Hamish Hamilton, 1974), p. 113.

Acknowledgements

All images reproduced with the kind permission of the copyright holders detailed below. All photographs of artworks from the author's collection by Toby Harries.

Page 6 The creation of the sun, moon and stars, twelfth-century mosaic, Monreale Cathedral, Palermo, Sicily (Granger Historical Picture Archive/Alamy Stock Photo).

Page 10 Jacopo Tintoretto, *Creation of the Animals*, 1551–52, Gallerie dell'Accademia, Venice (akg-images/Cameraphoto).

Page 14 Lucas Cranach the Elder, *Adam and Eve*, 1526, Courtauld Gallery, London (Heritage Images/Fine Art Images/akg-images).

Page 18 Masaccio, *The Expulsion from Eden*, c. 1425, Brancacci Chapel, Santa Maria del Carmine, Florence (akg-images/Rabatti & Domingie).

Page 24 Marc Chagall, *Exodus*, 1952, Musée National Marc Chagall, Nice (RMN-Grand Palais (Musée Marc Chagall)/Gérard Blot/ADAGP, Paris and DACS, London 2019).

Page 30 Moses before the Burning Bush, sixth-century mosaic, St Catherine's Monastery, Sinai (akg-images/Pictures From History).

Page 34 Albert Herbert, *Elijah Being Fed by a Raven*, 1992 (Estate of Albert Herbert, Private Collection/England & Co., London/Bridgeman Images).

Page 38 Holy Wisdom, sixteenth-century icon, Sophia Cathedral, Novgorod (The History Collection/Alamy Stock Photo).

Page 44 Roger Wagner, *And the Lord Lifted Up Job's Face*, 1995 (Roger Wagner).

Page 48 Patricia Fostiropoulos, Icon of loving kindness, 1990 (from the author's collection).

Page 52 Piero della Francesca, *The Baptism of Christ*, c. 1450, National Gallery, London (akg-images/WHA/World History Archive).

Page 56 Stanley Spencer, *The Scorpion*, 1939 (State Art Collection, Art Gallery of Western Australia, purchased 1983/Bridgeman Images)

Page 60 Rembrandt, *Christ Healing and Preaching*, c. 1648 (Artimages/Alamy Stock Photo).

Page 64 Hildegart Nicholas, *The Prodigal*, 1991, St Luke's Chapel, Royal Bournemouth Hospital, where the mosaic can be viewed (Chaplaincy Department, Royal Bournemouth and Christchurch Hospitals NHS Foundation Trust 2019).

Page 68 Edith Reyntiens, Icon of the Transfiguration after the prototype of Theophanes the Greek, c. 1986 (from the author's collection).

Page 72 Leonardo da Vinci, *The Last Supper*, c. 1494–98, Monastery of Santa Maria delle Grazie, Milan (Ian Dagnall/Alamy Stock Photo).

Page 76 Helen Meyer, *Agony in the Garden of Gethsemane*, c. 1990 (from the author's collection).

Page 80 Norman Adams, *The Golden Crucifixion*, 1993 (Benjamin Adams).

Page 84 The Anastasis, fourteenth-century fresco, Church of the Holy Saviour, Chora (Kariye Camii), Istanbul (akg-images/Rainer Hackenberg).

Page 88 The two Marys finding the tomb of Jesus empty, sixth-century mosaic, Basilica of Sant'Apollinare Nuovo, Ravenna (akg-images/Erich Lessing).

Page 94 David Wynne, *Noli me tangere* (Christ and Mary Magdalen), 1963, Magdalene College, Oxford (Estate of David Wynne. All rights reserved, DACS 2019/Mulrooney Oxford UK/Alamy Stock Photo).

Page 98 Mosaic at Hosios Loukas, Greece, *c.* 1120 (akg-images/Paul Ancenay).

Page 102 Ceri Richards, *The Supper at Emmaus*, 1958, Chapel of St Edmund Hall, Oxford (Estate of Ceri Richards. All rights reserved, DACS 2019/Photography: St Edmund Hall, Oxford).

Page 106 Caravaggio, *Conversion on the Way to Damascus*, 1600–02, Santa Maria del Popolo, Rome (incamerastock/Alamy Stock Photo).

Page 110 Nicholas Mynheer, *Worcester College Chapel Choir*, 2003 (Nicholas Mynheer).

Page 116 The dormition of the Blessed Virgin Mary, twelfth-century icon, Desyatinny Monastery, Novgorod (Picture Art Collection/Alamy Stock Photo).

Page 120 Tom Denny, Window in memory of Thomas Traherne, 2006–07, Hereford Cathedral (Tom Denny/Photography: James Davies).

Page 126 Solomon Raj, Etching, *c.* 1995 (from the author's collection).

Page 130 Fra Angelico, *Christ Glorified in the Court of Heaven*, altarpiece panel, *c.* 1423–24, Convent of San Domenico, Fiesole (Heritage Images/Fine Art Images/akg-images).

Page 136 Andrei Rublev, *The Trinity*, icon, *c.* 1425–27, Tretyakov Gallery, Moscow (akg-images/Pictures From History).